Building CI/CD Systems Using Tekton

Develop flexible and powerful CI/CD pipelines using Tekton Pipelines and Triggers

Joel Lord

BIRMINGHAM—MUMBAI

Building CI/CD Systems Using Tekton

Copyright © 2021 Packt Publishing

Group Product Manager: Vijin Boricha
Publishing Product Manager: Shrilekha Malpani
Senior Editor: Shazeen Iqbal
Content Development Editor: Romy Dias
Technical Editor: Shruthi Shetty
Copy Editor: Safis Editing
Project Coordinator: Shagun Saini
Proofreader: Safis Editing
Indexer: Vinayak Purushotham
Production Designer: Joshua Misquitta

First published: August 2021

Production reference: 1050821

Published by Packt Publishing Ltd.
Livery Place
35 Livery Street
Birmingham
B3 2PB, UK.

ISBN 978-1-80107-821-4

www.packt.com

To Mom, who taught me the importance of books, and to Dad, for bringing that Hyperion at home so many years ago.

Contributors

About the author

Joel Lord (`joel__lord` on Twitter) is passionate about the web and technology in general. He likes to learn new things, but most of all, he wants to share his discoveries. He does so by traveling to various conferences all across the globe.

He graduated from college with a degree in computer programming in the last millennium. Apart from a little break to get his BSc in computational astrophysics, he has always worked in the industry.

In his daily job, Joel is a developer advocate with MongoDB, where he connects with software engineers to help them make the web better by using best practices around JavaScript.

In his free time, he can be found stargazing on a campground somewhere or brewing a fresh batch of beer in his garage.

Before I started writing this book, I never realized how many people were involved in the process. So many people participated, making the end result what it is today. Big thanks to the team of illustrators, content editors, and technical reviewers. Special kudos to Romy Dias, who was a great help during the whole process. Most importantly, many thanks to my wonderful spouse, Natacha, for giving me the support I've needed to write this book.

About the reviewers

Jonas Pettersson is an independent software consultant with experience in different businesses and environments, from telecommunications to finance and start-ups. He is a software developer with experience mainly in Java-based environments. Over the last few years, he has been working in a Kubernetes-based platform team and has helped with continuous delivery and configuration management problems. Jonas has contributed to the Tekton project and is enthusiastic about the growing cloud-native landscape.

Brian Nguyen is an application architect and software engineer with a specialization in cloud-native applications and machine learning. Throughout his career, he has been responsible for entire software product developments, including collecting new requirements from the product manager, architecting custom solutions for the customer, and ensuring quality and security for the whole system. After several years in software development, in 2019, Brian joined Red Hat to work as an architect, where he is responsible for machine learning activities on the Kubernetes platform. Brian currently holds a Bachelor of Science in computer engineering from the University of Florida and a Master of Science in computer science from the Georgia Institute of Technology.

Table of Contents

Section 2: Tekton Building Blocks

3

Installation and Getting Started

4

Stepping into Tasks

5

Jumping into Pipelines

6

Debugging and Cleaning Up Pipelines and Tasks

7

Sharing Data with Workspaces

8

Adding when Expressions

9

Securing Authentication

Section 3: Tekton Triggers

10

Getting Started with Triggers

11
Triggering Tekton

Section 4: Putting It All Together

12
Preparing for a New Pipeline

13
Building a Deployment Pipeline

Assessments

Other Books You May Enjoy

Index

Preface

Tekton is a powerful yet flexible Kubernetes-native open source framework for creating **continuous integration and continuous delivery (CI/CD)** systems. It lets you build, test, and deploy across multiple cloud providers or on-premises systems by abstracting away the underlying implementation details.

Building CI/CD Systems Using Tekton covers everything you need to know to start building your pipeline and automate application delivery in a cloud-native environment. Using a hands-on approach, you will learn about the basic building blocks that you can use to compose your CI/CD pipelines. You will then learn how to use these components in conjunction with Tekton Triggers to automate the delivery of your application in a Kubernetes cluster.

By the end of this book, you will know how to compose Tekton Pipelines and use them with Tekton Triggers to build powerful CI/CD systems.

Who this book is for

This book caters to everyone who wants to learn about one of the most powerful Kubernetes-native CI/CD systems: Tekton. This book is aimed at software developers who want to use the **Custom Resource Definitions (CRDs)** in Kubernetes and use Tekton to run pipeline tasks in order to build and own application delivery pipelines.

What this book covers

Chapter 1, *A Brief History of CI/CD*, takes you a step back in time and explains where CI/CD comes from and why it is so important nowadays. This will help you understand the importance of building robust pipelines for quicker delivery of your application.

Chapter 2, *A Cloud-Native Approach to CI/CD*, explains that Tekton is different from other CI/CD solutions because of its cloud-native approach. In this chapter, you will learn what cloud-native development is and what it means in the context of CI/CD pipelines.

Chapter 3, *Installation and Getting Started*, explains how to prepare your environment for the exercises that will be presented in the book.

Chapter 4, Stepping into Tasks, explains that tasks are the basic building block of Tekton pipelines. They are at the heart of the Tekton philosophy. In this chapter, you will learn how to build and use tasks that are reusable.

Chapter 5, Jumping into Pipelines, explains that a Tekton pipeline is composed of multiple tasks. In this chapter, you will learn how to use the tasks you learned about in the previous chapter to build pipelines.

Chapter 6, Debugging and Cleaning Up Pipelines and Tasks, demonstrates that when authoring tasks, things don't always work as expected. This chapter introduces concepts to help find issues with Tekton pipelines and tasks. It also introduces a new concept called `finally`, which helps to clean up after a pipeline has been executed.

Chapter 7, Sharing Data with Workspaces, explains that in order to share data across the various tasks in a pipeline, there was originally a concept of pipeline resources. In the latest iteration of Tekton, workspaces are now the recommended way to do this.

Chapter 8, Adding when Expressions, explains that in order to add conditional statements in the execution of a pipeline, when expressions can be used. These expressions control the flow of the pipeline based on conditions.

Chapter 9, Securing Authentication, demonstrates that for certain operations, it is necessary to authenticate into a service. This can be done without exposing credentials by using secrets.

Chapter 10, Getting Started with Triggers, covers Tekton Triggers, a sister project of Tekton Pipelines that adds the ability to automatically trigger a pipeline by opening a route on your Kubernetes cluster and listening for incoming requests. In this chapter, you will learn about the new objects that are introduced by Tekton Triggers and how to install and prepare a local minikube cluster to listen for incoming requests.

Chapter 11, Triggering Tekton, explains how to create the required objects for the cluster to listen for a GitHub webhook and trigger a pipeline on certain actions.

Chapter 12, Preparing for a New Pipeline, prepares you to deploy a full real-world example of a Tekton pipeline. You will start by cleaning up the cluster and install all the required components on a fresh new installation of minikube. You will then be invited to explore the application that is about to be deployed. This will be a Node.js Express server with a few basic routes. Finally, you will be guided through the process of manually deploying and updating the application into the local cluster.

Chapter 13, Building a Deployment Pipeline, shows you how to build the tasks that are required for the pipeline and link them together. You will also need to create conditions, secrets, and workspaces to fully deploy the application.

To get the most out of this book

In order to use Tekton Pipelines, you will need access to a Kubernetes cluster. All the examples in this book are running on minikube. The installation instructions are provided in the book.

Software/hardware covered in the book	OS requirement
Kubernetes (minikube)	Windows, macOS, and Linux (any)
Tekton 0.20.1	Windows, macOS, and Linux (any)

If you are using the digital version of this book, we advise you to type the code yourself or access the code via the GitHub repository (link available in the next section). Doing so will help you avoid any potential errors related to the copying and pasting of code.

Download the example code files

You can download the example code files for this book from GitHub at `https://github.com/PacktPublishing/Building-CI-CD-systems-using-Tekton`. In case there's an update to the code, it will be updated on the existing GitHub repository.

We also have other code bundles from our rich catalog of books and videos available at `https://github.com/PacktPublishing/`. Check them out!

Code in Action

Code in Action videos for this book can be viewed at `https://bit.ly/2VmDYy0`.

Download the color images

We also provide a PDF file that has color images of the screenshots/diagrams used in this book. You can download it here: `http://www.packtpub.com/sites/default/files/downloads/9781801078214_ColorImages.pdf`.

Conventions used

There are a number of text conventions used throughout this book.

`Code in text`: Indicates code words in text, database table names, folder names, filenames, file extensions, pathnames, dummy URLs, user input, and Twitter handles. Here is an example: "Mount the downloaded `WebStorm-10*.dmg` disk image file as another disk in your system."

A block of code is set as follows:

```
apiVersion: apps/v1
kind: Deployment
...
  spec:
    containers:
```

When we wish to draw your attention to a particular part of a code block, the relevant lines or items are set in bold:

```
    - name: tekton-pod
      image: <YOUR_USERNAME>/tekton-lab-app
      ports:
      - containerPort: 3000
```

Any command-line input or output is written as follows:

```
$ kubectl apply -f ./deploy.yaml
deployment.apps/tekton-deployment created
service/tekton-svc created
ingress.networking.k8s.io/tekton-ingress created
```

Bold: Indicates a new term, an important word, or words that you see onscreen. For example, words in menus or dialog boxes appear in the text like this. Here is an example: "On the **Add webhook** screen on GitHub, fill in the form."

> **Tips or important notes**
> Appear like this.

Get in touch

Feedback from our readers is always welcome.

General feedback: If you have questions about any aspect of this book, mention the book title in the subject of your message and email us at customercare@packtpub.com.

Errata: Although we have taken every care to ensure the accuracy of our content, mistakes do happen. If you have found a mistake in this book, we would be grateful if you would report this to us. Please visit www.packtpub.com/support/errata, selecting your book, clicking on the Errata Submission Form link, and entering the details.

Piracy: If you come across any illegal copies of our works in any form on the Internet, we would be grateful if you would provide us with the location address or website name. Please contact us at copyright@packt.com with a link to the material.

If you are interested in becoming an author: If there is a topic that you have expertise in and you are interested in either writing or contributing to a book, please visit authors.packtpub.com.

Share your thoughts

Once you've read *Building CI/CD Systems Using Tekton*, we'd love to hear your thoughts! Scan the QR code below to go straight to the Amazon review page for this book and share your feedback.

https://packt.link/r/1801078211

Your review is important to us and the tech community and will help us make sure we're delivering excellent quality content.

Section 1: Introduction to CI/CD

This section serves as an introduction to **continuous integration and continuous** delivery (CI/CD), why they exist, and what they mean in the context of cloud-native development. You will start by learning about the history of the agile methodology and how it led to the creation of CI/CD principles.

Then, you will learn where Tekton fits into the CI/CD landscape. The main components that are used to create Tekton pipelines will be introduced to you.

By the end of this section, you will have an understanding of why you should be using CI/CD systems to automate your application delivery and where Tekton comes in to help you with CI/CD.

The following chapters will be covered in this section:

- *Chapter 1, A Brief History of CI/CD*
- *Chapter 2, A Cloud-Native Approach to CI/CD*

1
A Brief History of CI/CD

Application development has not always worked the way it does today. Not so long ago, the processes were much different, as was the available technology for software engineering. To understand the importance of **continuous integration/continuous deployment (CI/CD)**, it is essential to take a step back and see how it all started. In this chapter, you will learn how CI/CD came to where it is right now and where it might go in the future. You will take a small trip back in time – about 20 years ago – to see how application deployment was done back then, when I was still a junior developer. We will then look at various turning points in the history of software development practices and how this impacted the way we deploy applications today.

You will also learn about how cloud computing changed the way that we deliver software compared to how it was done about two decades ago. This will set the foundations for learning how to build powerful CI/CD pipelines with **Tekton**.

Finally, you will start to understand how CI/CD can fit into your day-to-day life as a software developer. Pipelines can be used at various stages of the application life cycle, and you will see some examples of their usage.

In this chapter, we are going to cover the following main topics:

- The early days
- Understanding the impacts of Agile development practices
- Deploying in the era of the cloud
- Demystifying CI versus CD versus CD

The early days

It doesn't seem that long ago that I had my first job as a software developer. Yet, many things have changed since. I still remember my first software release in the early 2000s. I had worked for months on software for our customer. I had finished all the requirements, and I was ready to ship all this to them. I burned the software and an installer on a CD-ROM; I jumped in my car and went to the customer's office. As you've probably guessed, when I tried to install the software, nothing worked. I had to go back and forth between my workplace and the customer's office many times before I finally managed to get it up and running.

Once the customer was able to test out the software, he quickly found that some parts of the software were barely usable. His environment was different and caused issues that I could not have foreseen. He found a few bugs that slipped through our QA processes, and he needed new features since his requirements had changed between the time he'd listed them and now.

I received the list of new features, enhancements, and bugs and got back to work. A few months later, I jumped into my car with the new CD-ROM to install the latest version on their desktop and, of course, nothing worked as expected again.

Those were the times of **Waterfall** development. We'll learn what this is about in the next section.

Waterfall model

The **Waterfall methodology** consists of a series of well-planned phases. Each phase required some thorough planning and that requirements were gathered. Once all these needs were established, shared with the customer, and well documented, the software development team would start working on the project. The engineers then deployed the software according to the specifications from the planning phase. Each of these cycles would vary in length but would typically be measured in months or years. Waterfall software development consists of one main phase, while agile development is all about smaller cycles based on feedback from the previous iteration.

The following diagram demonstrates the Waterfall methodology:

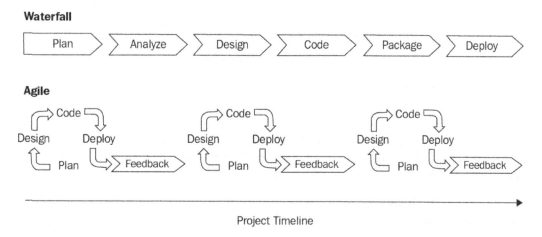

Figure 1.1 – Waterfall versus Agile

This model worked well on some projects. Some teams could do wonders using the Waterfall model, such as the *Apollo* space missions. They had a set of rigorous requirements, a fixed deadline, and were aiming for zero bugs.

In the early 2000s, though, the situation was quickly changing. More and more enterprises started to bloom on the internet and having a shorter time to market than the competition was becoming even more important. Ultimately, this is what led to the **agile manifesto** of 2001.

So far, you've learned how software development was done at the turn of the millennium. You've learned how those long cycles caused the releases to be spread apart. It sometimes took months, if not years, for two releases of a piece of software to be released. In the next section, you will see how agile methodologies completely revolutionized the way we build software.

Understanding the impacts of Agile development practices

At the same time as I was making all those round trips to my customer, a group of software practitioners met at a conference. These thinkers came out of this event with the foundation of what became the "*Agile Alliance*." You can find out more about the Agile Alliance and the manifesto they wrote at http://agilemanifesto.org.

The agile manifesto, which lists the main principles behind the methodology by the same name, can be summarized as follows:

- Individuals and interactions over processes and tools

- Working software over comprehensive documentation

- Customer collaboration over contract negotiation

- Responding to change over following a plan

Those principles revolutionized software engineering. It was a significant change from the Waterfall model, and it is now the method that's used for most modern software development projects.

Had **agile methodologies** been used when I originally wrote my first piece of software, there are many things I would have done differently.

First, I would have fostered working much more closely with my customer. Right from my first release, it was apparent that we had a disconnect in the project's vision. Some of the features that he needed were not implemented in a way that made sense for his day-to-day usage. Even though our team provided many documents and charts to him to explain what I was about to implement, it would have probably been easier to discuss how they were planning to use the software. Picking up a phone or firing off an email to ask a question will always provide a better solution than blindly following a requirements document. Nowadays, there is tooling to make it easier to collaborate more closely and get better feedback.

One part of the software that I delivered that made me immensely proud was an advanced templating engine that would let the customer automate a mail-out process. It used a particular syntax, and I provided a guide that was a few pages long (yes, a hard copy!) for the users to be able to use it. They barely ever used it, and I ultimately removed the engine in a future version favoring a hardcoded template. They filled in one or two fields, clicked **Submit**, and they were done. When the template needed to be changed, I would update the software, and within a few hours, they had a patch for the new template. In this specific case, it didn't matter how well-written my documentation was; the solution did not work for them.

This over-engineered feature is also a great example of where *customer collaboration* is so important. In this specific situation, had I worked more closely with the customer, I might have better understood their needs. Instead, I focused on the documentation that was prepared in advance and stuck to it.

Finally, there's responding to change over following a plan. Months would go by between my updates. In this day and age, this might seem inconceivable. The planning processes were long, and it was common practice to publish all the requirements beforehand. Not only that, but deploying software was a lot harder than it is nowadays. Every time I needed to push an update, I needed to meet with the system administrators a couple of weeks before the installation. This sysadmin would check the requirements, test everything out, and eventually prepare the desktop to receive the software's dependencies. On the day of installation, I needed to coordinate with the users and system administrators to access those machines. I was then able to install the latest version on their device manually. It required many people's intervention, and no one wanted me to come back in 2 days with a new update, which made it hard to respond to changes.

Those agile principles might seem like the norm nowadays, but the world was different back then. A lot of those cumbersome processes were required due to technological limitations. Sending large files over the internet was tricky, and desktop applications were the norm. It was also the beginning of what came to be known as *Web 2.0*. With the emergence of new languages such as PHP and ASP, more and more applications were being developed and deployed to the web.

It was generally easier to deploy applications to run on the web; it simply consisted of uploading files to an FTP server. It didn't require physical access to a computer and much fewer interactions with system administrators. The end users didn't need to update their application manually; they would access the application as they always would and notice a change in a feature or an interface. The interactions were limited between the software developers and the system administrators to get a new version of the application up and running.

Yet, the Waterfall mentality was still strong. More and more software development teams were trying to implement agile practices, but the application deployment cycle was still somewhat slow. The main reason for this was that they were scared of breaking a production build with an update.

Here be testing

Software engineers adopted many strategies to mitigate the risk associated with deploying a new version of the application. One such method was **unit testing** and **test-driven development**. With unit testing, software developers were able to run many tests on their code base, ensuring that the software was still working. By executing a test run, developers could be reassured that the new features they implemented didn't break a previously developed component.

Having those tests in place made it much easier to build in small iterations and show the changes to a customer, knowing that the software didn't suffer from any regressions. The customer was then able to provide feedback much earlier in the development loop. The development teams could react to those comments before they invested too much time in a feature that would end up not satisfying the users in the end.

It was a great win for the customers, but it also turned out to be a great way to help the system administrators. With software that was tested, there were much fewer chances of introducing regression in the current application. Sysadmins were more confident in the build and more willing to deploy the applications regularly. The processes were starting to become automated via some bash scripting by the administrators to facilitate the processes.

Still, some changes were harder to push. When changes needed to be made to a database or an upgrade was required for a runtime, operators were usually more hesitant to implement those changes. They would need to set up a new environment to test out the new software and ensure that those changes would not cause problems with the servers. That reality changed in 2006 when Amazon first introduced *AWS*.

Cloud computing was to technology what agile methodologies were to software development processes. The changes that they brought changed the way developers did their jobs. Now, let's dig deeper to see how the cloud impacted software engineering.

Deploying in the era of the cloud

The cloud brought drastic changes to the way applications were built and maintained. Until then, most software development shops or online businesses had their own servers and team to maintain said servers. With the advent of AWS, all of this changed. It was now possible to spin up a new environment and use that new environment directly on someone else's infrastructure. This new way of doing things meant less time managing actual hardware and the capability to create reproducible environments easily.

With what was soon known as **the cloud**, it was easier than ever to deploy a new application. A software developer could now spin up a virtual machine that had the necessary software and runtimes, and then execute a batch of unit tests to ensure that it was running on that specific server. You could also create an environment for the customers to see the application changes at the end of each iteration, which helped them approve those new features or provide feedback on a requested enhancement.

With server environments that were easier to start, faster to scale, and cheaper than actual hardware, more and more people moved to *cloud-based software development*. This move also facilitated the automation of many processes around software deployment practices. Using a command-line tool, it was now possible to start a new staging environment, spin up a new database, or take down a server that wasn't needed.

More and more companies were having a presence on the web, and the competition to get out new features or implement the same features as your competition became a problem. It was no longer acceptable to deploy every few months. If a competitor released a new feature, your product also needed to implement it as soon as possible due to the risk of losing a market share. If there was a delay in fixing a bug, that also meant a potentially significant revenue loss.

These fast changes were at the heart of a revolution in how teams worked to build and deploy applications. Until now, enterprises had teams of software engineers who oversaw designing new features, fixing bugs, and preparing the next releases. On the other hand, a group of system administrators oversaw that all the infrastructures were running smoothly and that no bugs were introduced in the system. Despite having the same goal of making the applications run better, those two teams ended up contradicting each other due to the nature of their work.

The programmers had pressure to release faster, but they would potentially introduce bugs or required software upgrades on the servers with each release. Sysadmins were under pressure to keep the environment stable and pushed changes to avoid breaking the fragile equilibrium in the systems in place. This dichotomy led to a new philosophy in enterprises: **DevOps**.

DevOps' idea was to bridge that gap between the two teams so that deploying better software quicker was finally possible. Lots of tools aim to make DevOps easier, and containers are one of those technologies.

Works on my machine!

One problem that has always existed is software engineering became more prevalent with the cloud – the "*Works on my machine*" syndrome. A programmer would install all the required software to run an application on their development machine, and everything ran smoothly. As soon as this software was shipped on a different device, though, everything stopped working.

This is a widespread problem at larger companies where multiple teams have various environments. A programmer would have *Apache 2.4* running *PHP 8.0*, while someone on the QA team would be running *Apache 2.3* with *PHP 7.2*. Both of those setups have benefits. The software developers tend to use the latest version available to benefit from all the new features that would make their life easier. On the other hand, the QA team would try to use the most common setup – the one where most of the customers would be.

This was also very true a few years ago when browsers differed from one vendor to the next. Software engineers were typically using Chrome or Firefox because they provided the best developer tools. In contrast, the testing team would use Internet Explorer because they still had the largest market share.

When teams had different environments, they would get mixed results when running the applications. Some features wouldn't work, or some bugs were raised that weren't reproducible by the developers. Trying to fix issues related to the environment is much more complicated than fixing problems that lie in the source code. You must compare the environment and understand why a specific piece of software did not behave as expected. Often, a note was added to the ticket mentioning either "*Works on my machine*" or "*Cannot reproduce*," and the ticket was closed without being fixed.

This type of scenario is prevalent between QA and software engineers and is present for system administrators and programmers. In the same way, developers typically used the latest versions of software, say a database, but the version running on the servers would be years old, so it would continue to support older applications.

A software engineer could request a newer version to be installed, but that was not a guarantee. Perhaps the more recent version had not been tested on the infrastructure. Maybe installing two different versions on a single machine was merely impossible. Either way, if the system administrators couldn't install the newer database, it meant going back to the drawing board, getting a development environment that ran the version installed on the servers, and getting it to work.

In 2013, a new startup came with a solution to those problems. **Container** technology was not new. In fact, process isolation, which is at the heart of how containers work, was introduced in 1979 in Unix V7. Yet, it was only close to 35 years later that it was made mainstream.

That startup was Docker. They built a tool that made it much easier for software engineers to ship their applications along with the whole environment.

If you are not familiar with containers, they are basically giant ZIP files that you would package your source code in, as well as the required configurations, the necessary runtimes, and so on. Essentially, programmers now shipped everything needed to run an application. The other benefit of containers is that they run in complete isolation from the underlying operating system.

With containers, it was finally possible to work in a development environment that was identical to the production or testing environments. Containers were the solution to the "*Works on my machine*" problem. Since all the settings were identical, the bugs had to be related to the source code and not due to a difference in the associated runtimes.

Scripting overload

Containers rapidly became a solution of choice for deploying applications in the cloud. The major cloud computing providers added support for them, making it more and more simple to use container technology.

The advent of containers was also a significant benefit to DevOps communities. Now, developers could pick the software they needed, and system operators didn't have to worry as much about breaking older legacy systems with newer versions.

Containers are intended to have minimal overhead. With a minimal set of resources, many of them can be started – much fewer resources than virtual machines, that is. The good thing about this is that we can break down large applications into smaller pieces called microservices.

Instead of having one extensive application deployed occasionally, software engineers started to break these down into smaller standalone chunks that would communicate with each other. With microservices, it was much easier to deploy applications faster. Smaller modules reduced the risk of breaking the whole application, and the impact of each deployment was smaller, making it possible to deploy more frequently.

Like every solution that seems too good to be true, microservices also came with their own set of problems. It turns out that, even with container technology, when an application has hundreds or even thousands of containers running simultaneously and communicating with each other, it can be challenging to manage. System administrators at large enterprises relied on scripting to manage those containers and ensure that they were up and running at any given time. A good understanding of the system was required, and those operators were doing a job similar to traffic controllers; that is, making sure that all those containers were working as they should and not crashing.

Google was an early adopter of container technology and was running thousands of them. They built a cluster manager called *Borg* to help them keep all those containers up and running. In 2014, they rewrote this project and released it as an open source project called *Kubernetes*.

Kubernetes is a container orchestration platform for containers. It ensures that containers are always up and running and takes care of the networking between them. It also helps with deployment as it introduces mechanisms that can redirect traffic during upgrades or distribute traffic between various containers for better release management.

Kubernetes is now the standard solution for container orchestration in large enterprises and is available from most cloud providers.

The cloud today – cloud native

20 years after my first application deployments, things have evolved quite a bit. Often, applications are running in the cloud. Tooling is easier than ever to deploy and manage such applications. We are now in the era of cloud-native software development.

There is no need to access a user's machine to release new software; it is possible to push these changes via the web directly. Even in software that runs locally, such as mobile applications or phone operating systems, upgrades are usually done seamlessly through automated processes.

This means constant application upgrades and security patches without the need for a manual process for the end user. These frequent upgrades keep your customers happier and more engaged with your product. If a user happens to find a bug, it can automatically be fixed quickly.

For enterprises, this means being able to push new features more quickly than the competition. With tooling such as unit testing, new builds are generally more reliable, and the risk of regressions is highly reduced. Even if a new feature would break the application in place, tools such as Kubernetes let your team quickly revert changes to an older state while waiting for a patch to be released.

For the software developers, this means less hassle when pushing a new version. System operators are more confident that the microservices won't interfere with other systems in place. With containers, the friction between the teams is also less frequent, and trust is higher regarding the software's quality.

Not only are the applications deployed to the cloud, but applications can also be tested, packaged, and even built directly with tooling that exists on the web. **Tekton** is one of those tools you can use in your server's infrastructure to manage your deployments.

The future of the cloud

Just like there was no way for me to predict the cloud 20 years ago, I can't predict what we will see in the future. One thing is certain, though: the cloud will stick around for many more years. The flexibility and ease of use that it brings to software development has helped software developers become more productive. Once all the tooling is in place, programmers can focus on their code and forget about all the hassle of deployment.

Already, we can see the emergence of cloud-based **IDEs**. It is possible to code directly in a web browser. This code is then pushed to a repository that lives on the web and can be automatically deployed to a cluster via some tools that exist "*as a Service.*"

These cloud-native tools will eventually bring even more uniformity across the environment and help software developers work even more closely to build better software.

So far, you've seen how the last 20 years have shaped the web as we now know it and the importance of deploying quicker and quicker. All of this brings us to our topic at hand: CI/CD.

Demystifying continuous integration versus continuous delivery versus continuous deployment

By using automation, it is possible to build more robust software and release it faster. Thanks to *containers* and *orchestration* platforms, it is also easier to build microservices that can be published with minimal impact on a larger system. These automation processes are generally known as **CI/CD**.

These processes are generally defined as three separate steps that compose a more extensive pipeline. These steps are **continuous integration**, **continuous delivery**, and **continuous deployment**.

The following diagram shows the various stages of CI/CD:

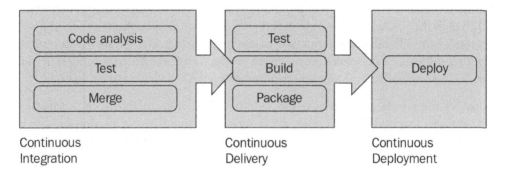

Figure 1.2 – Continuous integration / continuous delivery / continuous deployment

Let's take a look at each in more detail.

Continuous integration

The first step in the pipeline – **CI** – refers to **continuous integration**. This first automation process is typically meant for the developers and usually runs as part of the development environment.

In this step, the code is automatically analyzed to catch any issues that might come up before the application is released. Initially, this step mostly referred to running a series of unit tests, but it can now include many other processes. Those processes include (and are not limited to) the following:

- *Installing dependencies*: To validate all the code and check for potential vulnerabilities, the CI process would need to install all the project's dependencies.

- *Auditing for security vulnerabilities*: Once all the dependencies have been resolved, it is essential to check that each module from third-party vendors does not have security vulnerabilities. This process can be done automatically with various tools that match the current versions of those modules against a database of known security breaches.

- *Code linting*: Software developers tend to have their unique signatures. Think spaces versus tabs or single versus double-quotes. It is essential to have coding standards in a complex code base to increase code readability and reduce errors. Code linting will ensure the code that was written matches the defined standards for this application.

- *Type checking*: Many programming languages, such as JavaScript and PHP, are loosely typed. While the absence of typing can be a powerful feature of the language itself, it can also introduce hard-to-find bugs. To help find those bugs, some tools can be executed against source code to reveal potential flaws.

- *Unit testing*: To test out the business logic of the code, unit tests can be run on individual functions. The purpose of a unit test is only to validate the outcome of a single, standalone function. Those tests are generally quick and can be run against a large code base in a matter of seconds. Unit testing has been around since the 1960s but was popularized with the agile movement's rise in the early 2000s. Kent Beck, one of the fathers of the agile manifesto, was a prone supporter of writing tests before even writing code. This approach was known as **test-driven development** or **TDD**.

- *Merging*: Once all the code has been validated with the automated tools, the CI process can merge the code into a branch for a potential release to a staging environment.

The end goal of continuous integration is to automate and submit the code that an individual developer contributed to, to a shared repository. Once all the testing and code analysis has been performed, the code is trusted enough to be automatically merged. With automatic merges in place, the number of branches that need to be manually incorporated into the code base is smaller. This ultimately reduces the potential conflicts between various branches affecting the same code.

Continuous delivery

The **CD** component can be divided into two distinct steps. The first one, **continuous delivery**, refers to preparing an application to be delivered. It encapsulates all the steps required to prepare for application deployment. Those steps typically run for longer and are not necessarily executed every time there is a code change. Instead, they run automatically when some code is merged into a repository to prepare for the deployment. This could include doing the following:

- *Integration testing*: Once the business logic of each function has been tested, it's time to test that each component is working with the other as expected. This process, called integration testing, typically tests a real network response to see if the small units of software work as expected with an authentic response. Those tests usually run longer and are only performed for the components involved in the current development cycle.

- *E2E testing*: End-to-end testing (also known as E2E testing) tests all the user journeys in an application. These tests extend to the UI, all the way to the network responses from a backend. They take much longer to perform, but they can usually help find regression bugs by testing the application as a whole.

- *Compile and build*: When applications need to be compiled, such as mobile or native desktop applications, this needs to be done. The output would be an executable or package that can then be installed and tested out by a QA team or a customer to provide feedback.

- *Package and containerize*: With some applications, it makes sense to prepare a container for distribution. Building this container and pushing the resulting image to a registry would be done at this phase.

Ultimately, the result of the continuous delivery phase is to provide the team or the customers with a version that can be tried and tested quickly. Continuous delivery was created in response to slower application delivery, which used to rely on manual processes. With faster delivery comes faster feedback, which is the goal of agile methodologies.

Continuous deployment

Finally, it is possible to automate the whole process even more. Now that the application has been packaged and ready for release in the continuous delivery phase, why not go one step further and automate deploying into production automatically?

Depending on the definitions, continuous deployment will often be part of the continuous delivery stage, but some people prefer to split those two to emphasize the amount of automation that can happen.

The deployment can take multiple forms and can be further automated using **blue/green deployment** methods, as an example.

CI/CD in the real world

Most software engineering teams will use some automation processes to help with their application delivery, usually referred to as CI/CD. The amount of automation they use can vary greatly. Some enterprises will only automate processes in the development environment. In contrast, others will automate the whole process and deploy to production as soon as a change has been pushed to a repository. The series of steps that are performed as part of that CI/CD process is called the pipeline.

In this book, you will learn how to build some of those pipelines using **Tekton** to automate your own processes. These examples will provide you with some simple to understand concepts, and will also help you eventually migrate to more practical examples that can be used in your regular responsibilities as a software developer.

Summary

In this first chapter, you learned about the importance of deploying applications faster. By building your CI/CD pipelines, you can integrate processes such as code linting or E2E testing as part of your automated processes to ensure that your applications are more robust.

In the next chapter, you will learn what CI/CD means in the context of cloud native and learn about some of the basic concepts that are used in Tekton.

2
A Cloud-Native
Approach to CI/CD

In the first chapter, we took a trip down memory lane to see how software engineering evolved to where it is today – that is, to the days of *cloud-native software development*. However, cloud-native is still a vague term that does not seem to have a fixed definition.

In this chapter, you will learn about what it means to build software in the context of **cloud-native**. You will learn about how this differs from traditional software development.

Once you have a better understanding of what cloud-native means, we will see how this applies to **CI/CD**. To do so, we will look at some of the benefits provided to us by cloud-native principles and try to apply them to CI/CD.

These principles will lead us to **Tekton**. In this chapter, you will learn what Tekton's mission is and how it fits into cloud-native strategies. You will then learn about the basic components that can be used to build Tekton **pipelines** and how they all work together.

By the end of this chapter, you will have a good understanding of the components that can be used to build CI/CD pipelines with Tekton, and you will be ready to jump into some concrete examples.

In this chapter, we're going to cover the following main topics:

- Being a software developer in the age of cloud-native development
- Understanding cloud-native CI/CD
- Introducing Tekton
- Exploring Tekton's building blocks
- Understanding TaskRuns and PipelineRuns

Being a software developer in the age of cloud-native development

Chances are that you've had to deal with the cloud at some point or another in your career already, but does that make you a cloud-native software developer? The term cloud-native can be overloaded. There are many definitions out there, and it's usually more of a range than an actual set of criteria.

For all things cloud-native-related, we can look toward the **Cloud Native Computing Foundation**, also known as the **CNCF** (https://www.cncf.io). The CNCF is a vendor-neutral home for open source projects that are related to cloud-native technologies. They host projects such as Kubernetes, **containerd**, and **Prometheus**.

In 2018, they came up with the following definition:

"Cloud-native technologies empower organizations to build and run scalable applications in modern, dynamic environments such as public, private, and hybrid clouds. Containers, service meshes, microservices, immutable infrastructure, and declarative APIs exemplify this approach.

These techniques enable loosely coupled systems that are resilient, manageable, and observable. Combined with robust automation, they allow engineers to make high-impact changes frequently and predictably with minimal toil."

(from https://github.com/cncf/toc/blob/master/DEFINITION.md)

The first step into cloud-native software development is making your application compliant with the **Twelve-Factor App** methodology. If you want to find out more about what those 12 factors are, you can take a look at the respective website at `https://12factor.net`.

Restating what is in their website in a nutshell, this methodology will show you how to build applications that do the following:

- Make onboarding new developers easier with the help of automation, such as CI/CD.

- Can be ported across various operating systems and execution environments using container technology.

- Can be deployed directly to the cloud using a DevOps mindset and avoid us having to rely on a center of excellency to manage the systems.

- Reduce the differences across the various environments such as development, staging, and production to make it easier to use CD principles.

- Can be scaled up or down without this having an impact on the other nodes in the system.

Using containerization technologies is a step in the right direction as it will allow you to build applications that are portable and scalable. You will be able to deploy such an application quickly on most of the major cloud providers.

In addition to packaging up applications in a container, you can also start using some tooling that runs in containers. These containerized environments make it easier for a distributed team to work with the same tools to ensure that development is cohesive.

Eventually, all development can be done directly from inside containers. These containers would include a development environment and can be shared with all the team members.

In the next section, you will learn how to apply cloud-native software development principles to CI/CD pipelines.

Understanding cloud-native CI/CD

Now that you have a better understanding of what cloud-native software development means, let's see what it means in the context of CI/CD pipelines.

Cloud-native CI/CD is based on three principles:

- **Containers**
- **Serverless**
- **DevOps**

Let's look at each of them in more detail.

Containers

Cloud-native, in the context of CI/CD, means that everything should be running inside containers. Each operation that's completed on a code base to test or package up the application should be done in its own isolated container.

Using those containers ensures that any team member or automated system can execute the same operation and get the same predictable end result.

This also means that all the runtimes and configurations needed to run a specific task on some source code will always be the same each time the pipeline runs. This ensures more stability in the pipelines, and you don't need a system administrator's help to install the necessary tooling.

Serverless

When we're talking about cloud-native CI/CD, serverless does not refer to **Functions as a Service** such as *Azure Functions* or *AWS Lambdas*. It is about running and scaling on demand, without the need for a central CI engine to be maintained and taken care of.

As a software developer, you should be able to edit and run your pipelines within your resource allocation, efficiently and promptly. You shouldn't need to have administrator privileges in a central system that manages your pipelines. For a cloud-native CI/CD solutions to be successful, it needs to be accessible and manageable by all the system users.

DevOps

Finally, cloud-native CI/CD needs to be built with DevOps practices in mind. It should allow teams to own their delivery pipelines, alongside the application, without relying on a central center of excellence team that manages delivery pipelines on another team's behalf.

Making the software development team responsible for their pipelines ensures they can manage them and always use the latest required software to do their job.

These are the principles that led to Tekton being created, a cloud-native CI/CD solution that runs on Kubernetes natively. In the next section, you will learn more about Tekton and how it approached CI/CD with a cloud-native mindset.

Introducing Tekton

When you look at CI/CD solutions, they all aim to do the same thing. Essentially, you provide a pipeline with an input (typically, this is your source code), and you get an output at the end (typically, this is a packaged application).

The steps that are performed on your inputs can vary from one project to another, but the same ones can also be used across all your projects. Think of actions such as `git clone`. Chances are, this will almost always be the first step in your pipeline.

The main goal of Tekton is to provide a cloud-native standard set of building blocks for CI/CD systems to make it easier and faster to build, test, and package up your source code. It runs on Kubernetes and can target any platform, any language, and any cloud.

The Tekton project's vision is to create a set of composable, declarative, reproducible, and cloud-native components that can be used to develop robust pipelines. Because Tekton adds a set of **Custom Resource Definitions (CRD)**, it is possible to reuse your pipelines or parts of those pipelines across multiple clouds.

Custom Resource Definitions (CRDs)

CRDs are an easy way to extend the Kubernetes API. Simply put, it is a way to create new objects that would extend the original Kubernetes scope. By creating those objects, it is possible to create software that runs directly inside Kubernetes, such as Tekton. To find out more about CRD, you can look at the Kubernetes documentation at `https://kubernetes.io/docs/concepts/extend-kubernetes/api-extension/custom-resources/`.

The following diagram sums up the four principles that guide Tekton's vision:

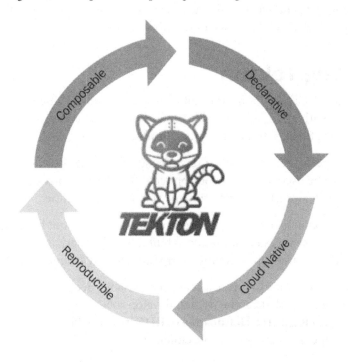

Figure 2.1 – Tekton's vision

Tekton is an open source project, and you can find all the related code repositories under their GitHub organization at `http://github.com/tektoncd`. You will notice that many individuals are involved in the project and that it is also backed by some major companies such as Red Hat, Google, IBM, Alibaba, and many more.

As we mentioned earlier Tekton is a collection of CRDs, but it also includes many smaller projects such as the Tekton **CLI**, **Triggers**, **Catalog**, and **Dashboard**.

In the next few sections, we'll take a closer look at each of these.

Tekton CLI

As the name implies, the **Tekton CLI** is the CLI tool that is used to manage Tekton pipelines. This tool makes it easier to interact with Tekton components and is better than relying on **kubectl**. It is available as a binary for all the major operating systems and can be installed directly from the source code.

You can find the source code for this tool, as well as all its releases, in the Tekton GitHub repository at `https://github.com/tektoncd/cli`.

This tool's installation instructions and usage will be covered in the next chapter of this book.

Tekton Triggers

Tekton Triggers appeared as a child project of Tekton. It allows users to add a way to launch pipelines based on **webhooks** automatically. A typical use case for this would be to add your Tekton Trigger URL to your GitHub repository. This URL would be reached each time an event occurs. Events would include things such as code pushes.

Using Triggers, you can launch a pipeline each time a `git push` is done in your code base. GitHub will then send a `POST` request to your cluster with a payload containing all the information about the event, such as the repository's URL and the branch name. Based on this payload, you can trigger various pipelines if needed. For example, you could start the pipeline so that it deploys the application to production each time new code is merged into the master branch.

You can find out more information about Tekton Triggers, along with its source code, on GitHub at `https://github.com/tektoncd/triggers`.

Tekton Triggers will be covered in the third part of this book.

Tekton Catalog

One of the goals of Tekton is to make *Tasks* as reusable as possible, so you don't have to reinvent the wheel each time you need to create a new pipeline. Tekton provides a set of standardized tasks that you can use on any of your CI/CD pipelines to help you with this.

Using an example that we discussed previously, you would almost always perform a `git clone` task at the beginning of your pipeline to fetch the source code from a repository. A premade task, managed by the Tekton team, can be installed directly into your cluster so that you can use this task out of the box. These tasks have undergone much testing and will allow you to reuse them in all your projects.

You can find the code for the actual Catalog at `https://github.com/tektoncd/hub`, while all the available tasks are available in their own repository at `https://github.com/tektoncd/catalog`.

Some of these tasks will be used in the last part of this book, when we start building real-world examples of pipelines.

Tekton Dashboard

The newest addition to the Tekton project is its Dashboard. Once it's been set up in your cluster, it will provide you with a web-based UI so that you can view and manage your Tekton components. It is built with **React**, and it can be installed directly into your Kubernetes cluster. You can find the source code for this project on GitHub at `https://github.com/tektoncd/dashboard`.

An overview of the Dashboard will be introduced in *Chapter 3*, *Installation and Getting Started*.

These different projects might seem like a lot of content to cover, but we will slowly introduce each of these new tools throughout this book. Before we start working with these side projects, we need to understand what a Tekton Pipeline is.

Exploring Tekton's building blocks

We are almost ready to get started with some hands-on examples of how to use Tekton, but before we do so, it is crucial to understand the basic **building blocks** that are used to build Tekton pipelines.

There are not many components that can be used to build pipelines in Tekton, but they can all be parameterized and tweaked to build powerful pipelines. In this section, we will explore all of them and see how they fit together.

Steps, tasks, and pipelines

The components you will be using the most when dealing with Tekton pipelines are **steps**, **tasks**, and **pipelines**. You can see the relationship between each of them in the following diagram:

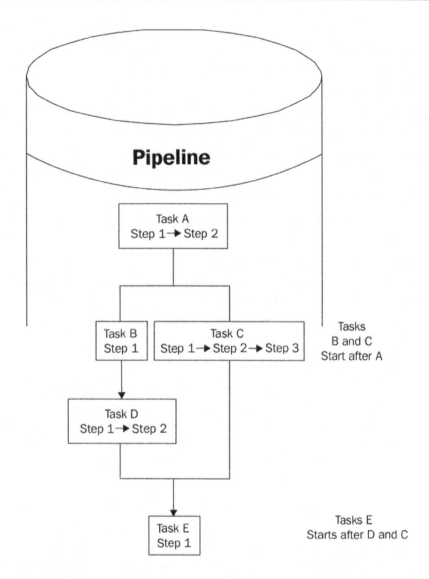

Figure 2.2 – Steps, tasks, and pipelines (http://tekton.dev/concepts)

To get a better understanding of how they work together, let's look at them individually.

Steps

Steps are the most basic units that you can use to create your pipeline. They represent a single operation that is part of your greater CI/CD process. Examples of a step could be running a test suite or compiling an application.

Each step runs in its own container. Once this step is completed, the container is taken down, and everything inside it will be lost unless it's stored in a shared volume.

Using a container for each step is a great way to ensure that your steps will always be reproducible. Since they always run in the same environment, you can be confident that the output will be the same when you use the same inputs.

For each step, you will need to specify the image to be used and the command to be executed once this image is started.

The steps follow the Kubernetes container specification. If you are familiar with the Kubernetes syntax, you will find that writing your steps' descriptions is very similar to writing a pod template in Kubernetes.

Steps are used to compose **tasks**.

Tasks

A task is a collection of steps that will run in sequence. The steps inside a single task should be related to each other. They typically represent a single operation that has to be performed on the inputs. A more complex task could have multiple steps to prepare the environment for the larger task. An example would be a test suite that needs some dependencies before running. Installing these dependencies and running the test suites would be two distinct steps in a single task.

The task will run in a single **pod**, which enables your steps to share a common volume and some resources.

You can configure tasks in many ways. The most common configuration is to add multiple parameters. Adding those parameters to your tasks will let you reuse the same task in a different context.

You can find some pre-written tasks in the *Tekton Catalog*. Tasks for everyday operations such as `git clone` or `s2i` are available and supported by the Tekton team. Those tasks are good examples of more complex processes that have many parameters for maximum reusability in all your pipelines.

While you can use tasks by themselves, they are usually used to build larger **pipelines**.

Pipelines

A pipeline is a collection of tasks that will perform a series of operations on an input and potentially provide you with some output. Pipelines describe your CI/CD workflow. A typical pipeline would clone your code, run your tests, build an image, and deploy your application into a cluster.

A pipeline will create several Kubernetes pods and run them in an order specified by the user. They could be executed simultaneously for a faster output or sequentially if the task's output is required for the next one to be completed.

Like tasks, you can parameterize pipelines so that you can reuse them in different contexts. For example, a pipeline that takes a code base as input and pushes the resulting image to a cluster could be used in various projects, if the code repository and image name have been parameterized.

If a task is unsuccessful, the pipeline could be halted. This early stop is handy if you have a task that runs a test suite. It could prevent pushing a bugged image into production.

Where to use a step, a task, or a pipeline

A step is the smallest unit available to build your Tekton CI/CD pipelines. It should only do one thing. If you have multiple commands being executed in the context of a step, this is a sign that you should probably convert it into a task.

When writing a task, you should always keep reusability in mind. If a task becomes too complicated and contains too many steps, consider breaking it down into multiple tasks and join them inside a pipeline. Tasks can also have a single step if that is what makes the most sense for that case. A task that you wish to deploy to a cluster, for example, would probably have a single step that would use kubectl to deploy the image.

Pipelines are your CI/CD workflows. They will take an input and perform various tasks on it. In some cases, you'll only want to perform continuous integration. Here, you can perform tasks such as running tests and validating that the code has been audited. Typically, though, you must build a pipeline that can also perform the continuous deployment part and push a final package to a cluster. These complete pipelines are the type of CI/CD workflows that we will be focusing on in this book.

Workspaces

In the alpha version of Tekton, there was a concept called **Pipeline resources**. The idea behind it was that a pipeline would take an input and produce an output. Those inputs and outputs were defined as their own objects and could be interchanged across pipelines.

Pipeline resources didn't make it to the beta version, though. Instead, it is recommended that you use **Workspaces**. A Workspace is a shared volume that can be used across all the tasks running in your pipeline. The main benefit of using a shared volume is that any action that's performed on your source code, such as installing dependencies, will be persisted when other tasks access this same volume.

There are different types of workspaces. However, we will be focusing on *Persistent Volume Claims* in this book. Understanding how Kubernetes persists data across volumes is outside the scope of this book, but you can find more information on the topic on the Kubernetes documentation website at `https://kubernetes.io/docs/concepts/storage/persistent-volumes/`.

When using Workspaces, you have to be more aware of the sequence that your tasks will run in. If you clone a code repository, it will be your responsibility to ensure that this task is completed before you run another task that would download your code dependencies – more on that in *Chapter 7, Sharing Data with Workspaces*.

You can use Workspaces at the task level to add a shared volume across the various steps or at the pipeline level. All the steps from all the tasks will then have access to this Workspace.

Due to the nature of Workspaces, you will need to use a **TaskRun** or a **PipelineRun** to make this filesystem available to your task or pipeline.

In the next section, you will learn how TaskRuns and PipelineRuns relate to *tasks* and *pipelines*.

Understanding TaskRuns and PipelineRuns

TaskRuns and **PipelineRuns** represent how their counterparts are executed; that is, the *task* and the *pipeline*. They hold the current status of the task's and pipeline's execution and provide you with more information on their performance, as shown in the following diagram:

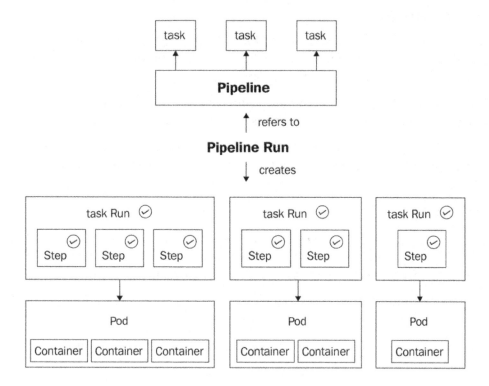

Figure 2.3 – PipelineRuns (http://tekton.dev/docs/concepts)

Here, you can see the tasks and pipelines that can be defined as templates so that they can be executed. When you use the CLI to start a pipeline (or a task), it will create the associated run.

TaskRuns

A TaskRun is used to execute a task on a cluster. While the task describes the operation that needs to happen in your pipeline, TaskRun describes this task's execution.

A TaskRun will execute all the steps in the task. It will also contain the status of the task's execution and the status of the execution of each step.

The TaskRun will execute until all the steps have been marked as successful.

PipelineRuns

PipelineRun is the pipeline version of a TaskRun. It represents how the pipeline is executed. The order in which the tasks will be executed as part of the PipelineRun will be determined by how it was specified in the pipeline.

When a PipelineRun is started, it automatically creates a TaskRun for each task in the associated pipeline. It will then contain the status of each of those TaskRuns.

The primary use for PipelineRuns is to be able to monitor the execution of your pipelines. They are used in dashboards to indicate the progress and completion of CI/CD pipelines.

Summary

In this chapter, you looked at the various building blocks that you can use to build your Tekton CI/CD pipelines. There aren't many components that you can use, but you will learn how to develop sturdy pipelines with them in the next few chapters.

Now that you know what steps, tasks, pipelines, and workspaces are, it is time to build our pipelines.

In the next chapter, you will learn how to install the necessary tooling to run Tekton and then jump into some hands-on examples.

Section 2: Tekton Building Blocks

This section is all about hands-on experience with the Tekton building blocks. Using concrete examples, you will learn everything you need to build powerful and flexible CI/CD systems using Tekton Pipelines.

First, you will start by installing all the necessary tools and configuring your Kubernetes cluster so that it is ready to run your Tekton pipelines. If you already have an environment ready, feel free to skip that chapter.

Once you have a local cluster ready to be used, you will explore the basic concepts that are needed to build your pipelines. Those building blocks are called Tasks and Pipelines.

With the hands-on examples provided so far, you will be ready to explore more advanced features. You will learn how to use shared volumes and how to clean them up. You will also learn how to add conditional statements and authentication to the components that will compose your pipelines.

By the end of this section, you will have all the necessary tools to start building your own Tekton pipelines.

The following chapters are included in this section:

3

Installation and Getting Started

Now that you have a better understanding of what cloud-native **continuous integration/ continuous deployment (CI/CD)** pipelines are all about, it's time to get your hands dirty and start exploring **Tekton**. In order to use Tekton locally, there are some tools that you will need on your computer.

In this section of the book, you will learn how to set up everything you need to navigate the exercises in the book. The first step will be to configure your development environment. As a software developer, you probably have most of the required tooling already installed, but it's still a good idea to take a minute to ensure this is the case.

Next, you will need to install the appropriate container runtime to run some of the hands-on examples provided in this book.

Once you have everything locally installed, you will also need a **Kubernetes** cluster in which Tekton will live. There are many options available to you. In this section, you will see how to install minikube, a tiny distribution of Kubernetes that runs locally.

Finally, you will see how to install the Tekton **custom resource definitions (CRDs)** on your cluster and install the **command-line interface (CLI)** tool needed to access those resources. Once this is done, you will be ready to get started with your Tekton Pipelines.

In this chapter, we're going to cover the following main topics:

- Setting up a developer environment
- Installing a container runtime and setting up a registry
- Picking a Kubernetes distribution (local, cloud, hosted)
- Connecting to your Kubernetes cluster
- Preparing the Tekton tooling

Technical requirements

Check out the following link to see the Code in Action video: `https://bit.ly/3BIR5tO`

Setting up a developer environment

While this book is not specifically about coding, there will still be code samples that are used from time to time. While it is not specifically necessary to understand and execute those code samples, it can be interesting to do so. The following tools will let you run those samples on your local machine.

All of the **YAML Ain't Markup Language** (YAML) files that are described in this book also appear in a shared Git repository (more details on this in the next section). In order to access these files, using Git and **Visual Studio Code** (**VS Code**) will make it easier for you.

Git

The first tool that you will need is **Git**. Git is a code versioning system that is free and open source. Developers use this tool to store source code in a common place and view the history of all code changes. It is used in most software engineering teams as a standard way to collaborate on a joint project.

To install Git, you can go to `https://git-scm.com/downloads` and pick your operating system, as shown in the following screenshot:

Figure 3.1 – Installing Git

If you are using a **Windows** operating system, it will automatically start a file download. Open this file to begin the installation process. The website will redirect you to a page with the installation instructions for your operating system for **macOS** and **Linux**.

Once you have Git installed, you can immediately clone the repository that holds all the examples from this book by running the following command:

```
$ git clone https://github.com/PacktPublishing/Building-CI-CD-
systems-using-Tekton.git
```

Node.js

JavaScript is truly everywhere nowadays. You will find it in your browser, of course, but also on backends and **Internet of Things (IoT)** devices. It has even made its way into this book. The few code samples that you will use in this book are written in JavaScript.

Node.js is a free and open source JavaScript runtime that will let you run some JavaScript code directly on your computer, without the need for an actual browser.

If you are not familiar with Node.js or even JavaScript, don't worry about it. The code samples used in this book are trivial, and understanding the code is not necessary to comprehend how Tekton works. Those code samples will be running inside containers, so you technically shouldn't even need to install this runtime.

If you do want to execute the code samples locally, though, you will need to install Node.js. You can find the installation instructions at `https://nodejs.org`, as shown in the following screenshot:

Node.js® is a JavaScript runtime built on Chrome's V8 JavaScript engine.

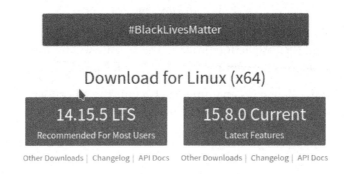

Figure 3.2 – Installing Node.js

The web page should provide you with a link to download for your operating system automatically. If the version differs from what you see in *Figure 3.2*, take the **Long-Term Support (LTS)** version.

To test that Node.js is installed locally and is working correctly, you can try the following in your terminal:

```
$ node -e "console.log('Hello world')"
```

You should then see the following output:

```
Hello world
```

VS Code

Code editors are a divisive topic among software developers. You can pick the one you want for the examples in this book. The choice of **integrated development environment (IDE)** won't matter, but I prefer **VS Code** because of its extension ecosystem.

With VS Code, you can find extensions to make you more productive in just about any coding language, including YAML files.

Here are some instructions on how to install VS Code and some of the extensions that I highly recommend installing to help you with your Tekton Pipelines.

To install VS Code, you can go to `https://code.visualstudio.com/`. There should be a button on the main page with a link to download the version for your operating system, as shown in the following screenshot:

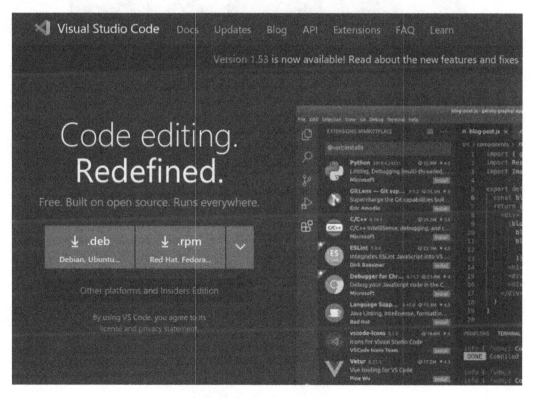

Figure 3.3 – Installing VS Code

Installing the extensions

To install extensions, you can open the **Extensions** panel in VS Code with *Ctrl + Shift + X*. From here, you can search for and install the following extensions:

- Kubernetes (`ms-kubernetes-tools.vscode-kubernetes-tools`) by Microsoft

- **YAML** (`redhat.vscode-yaml`) by Red Hat

- **Tekton Pipelines** (`redhat.vscode-tekton-pipelines`) by Red Hat

To install the extensions, click on the **Install** button, as shown in the following screenshot:

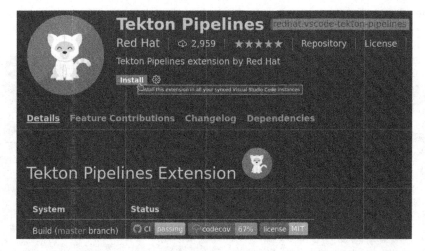

Figure 3.4 – Installing the Tekton Pipelines extension in VS Code

Now that you have a running developer environment, it's time to start adding the necessary tooling to containerize and deploy your application.

Installing a container runtime and setting up a registry

In some of the examples in this book, and to install **minikube** later, you will need to pick a runtime to run containers. There are many different options available to you. In this section, we will focus on the most popular choice, which is Docker.

The specific usage of containers is outside the scope of this book, but you can find more information about containers in a presentation by yours truly at `http://ezurl.to/containers`.

Docker

Docker, from the eponymous company, is the most popular option out there. This is especially true if you are using a Windows or macOS operating system. To run containers, you technically have to use a Linux operating system. Docker will take care of creating a **virtual machine** (**VM**) and will run the containers in there.

You can install Docker by visiting their **Getting Started with Docker** page at `https://docker.com/get-started`. From there, you can download the executable for your operating system, as demonstrated in the following screenshot:

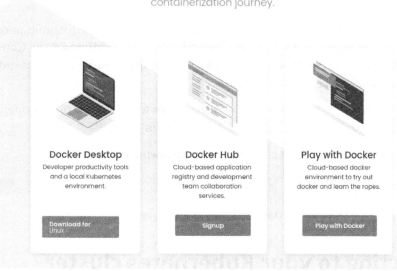

Figure 3.5 – Installing Docker and signing up for Docker Hub

To verify the installation of Docker, you can run the following command:

```
$ docker version
```

Docker Hub

While you are on the Docker **Get Started with Docker** page, you can also sign up for a free **Docker Hub** account. This account will give you access to a **container registry**. A registry is to containers what a repository is to code. It is a central place to store and share your containers. You will need access to such a registry in the later parts of this book, and Docker Hub is free and easy to use.

Picking a Kubernetes distribution (local, cloud, hosted)

Tekton runs inside a Kubernetes **cluster**, so to do any of the exercises in this book, you will need access to such a cluster. Many options can run locally on your machine or in the cloud, and range from free to thousands of **US dollars** (**USD**) per month.

If you already have a Kubernetes cluster available to you, feel free to skip this section and use your own.

If you do need access to your own Kubernetes cluster to experiment with the examples from this book, I recommend using a Kubernetes distribution that runs locally.

minikube

The easiest way to get started with Kubernetes is by running a micro distribution on your computer. There are many micro distributions available, such as **MicroK8s** by Canonical and **K3s** by Rancher. The one that will be used here is by the **Cloud Native Computing Foundation** (**CNCF**) and is called **minikube**.

You will find the download and installation instructions for minikube on any operating system at `https://minikube.sigs.k8s.io/docs/start/`.

Once it's installed, you can start a cluster with the following command:

```
$ minikube start
```

You'll then have a Kubernetes cluster running on your personal computer.

Connecting to your Kubernetes cluster

To interact with your Kubernetes cluster, you will need a CLI tool called **kubectl**. If you've already interacted with a Kubernetes cluster, you are most likely familiar with this tool. If you don't have it installed already, you can go to the Kubernetes official website and follow your operating system's installation instructions. You can find all the information needed for the `kubectl` installation at `https://kubernetes.io/docs/tasks/tools/install-kubectl/`.

Once the tool has been installed, you can test it out with the following command:

```
$ kubectl version
```

This command should output the current version of `kubectl`.

You will also need to configure kubectl to use your existing cluster. If you are using minikube, you can restart your cluster. When using minikube start, it will automatically configure kubectl for you.

For minikube, type the following command:

```
$ minikube stop && minikube start
```

If you are using a cloud-based Kubernetes distribution, you might need to look up your provider's documentation. Most cloud providers will provide you with a CLI tool specific to their platform that can be used to configure kubectl. For example, if you are using IBM Cloud, you will need the ibmcloud CLI tool and then use the following commands to configure kubectl:

```
$ ibmcloud login -a cloud.ibm.com -r us-south -g
$ ibmcloud ks cluster config --cluster <cluster_id>
```

Amazon Web Services (AWS), **Google**, **Azure**, and **DigitalOcean** all have similar tools to configure kubectl with their servers. Once kubectl is configured for your cluster, you can verify the cluster that it is connected to with the following commands, which should return the cluster for which it has been configured:

```
$ kubectl config current-context
$ kubectl cluster-info
```

With kubectl, you will be able to manage everything that is happening inside your cluster. Now that you have all the necessary tooling, you can start installing Tekton and the related tooling.

Preparing the Tekton tooling

Now that you have all the necessary tooling to run Tekton, it's time to get started with Tekton itself. The first step will be to install one final CLI tool to interact with Tekton. You can find this tool along with the installation instructions for your operating system at https://tekton.dev/docs/getting-started/#set-up-the-cli. If you prefer, you can also find the latest release directly on the **GitHub repository** at https://github.com/tektoncd/cli/releases/tag/v0.16.0.

Throughout this book, I will be using version 0.16.0 of the client.

You are now done with the installation of all the required tooling that will be needed for this book and to interact with any Tekton pipeline. The next step will be to install Tekton on your Kubernetes cluster. This command will install all the CRDs to be able to run Tekton **Tasks** and **Pipelines**. To install Tekton from your command line, use kubectl to fetch and install the latest release, as follows:

```
$ kubectl apply --filename https://storage.googleapis.com/
tekton-releases/pipeline/latest/release.yaml
```

If you are using an OpenShift cluster, you will need to use a slightly different command to install Tekton on your cluster. This is due to the way **CRI-O** tags images (where **CRI** stands for **Container Runtime Interface**). The command can be seen in the following code snippet:

```
$ kubectl apply --filename https://storage.googleapis.com/
tekton-releases/pipeline/latest/release.notags.yaml
```

Now that you have everything installed, try to run the following command:

```
$ tkn version
```

You should see your client version and the pipeline version that is currently running on your cluster. I will be using version 0.20.1 of Tekton for the purpose of this book.

If you are using a *nix-based operating system such as Linux or macOS, you can also install the autocompletion scripts. This will let you use <tab> to complete various commands, which is a nice tip to be more productive. To see how you can install the autocompletion tools, you can run the following command:

```
$ tkn completion --help
```

Tekton Dashboard

In this book, we will be almost exclusively using the CLI tool, but it is interesting to note that there is a **dashboard** available for Tekton. If you want to use the **graphical user interface (GUI)** for Tekton, you can install it by applying the YAML file for the latest release on your cluster, as follows:

```
$ kubectl apply --filename https://github.com/tektoncd/
dashboard/releases/latest/download/tekton-dashboard-release.
yaml
```

Once the pods are started and running, you can open a port to access the dashboard directly using the following command:

```
$ kubectl --namespace tekton-pipelines port-forward svc/tekton-dashboard 9097:9097
```

You can now open up your browser at `http://localhost:9097`, and you will see **Tekton Dashboard**, as shown in the following screenshot:

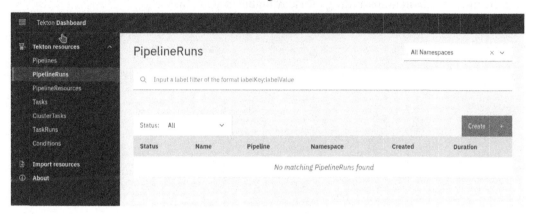

Figure 3.6 – Tekton Dashboard

There is not much content there for now, but don't worry—we will add to it.

Summary

That's it! You are now ready to get started with Tekton. In this chapter, you've installed all the necessary tools that you will need to follow along with the hands-on examples provided in this book.

You've set up your development environment with tools to run the Node.js examples that will be presented. You can also clone the source code from this book's repository now that you have Git installed. Additionally, you now have a code editor equipped with powerful plugins that will make it easier for you to build your Tekton Pipelines.

You've also configured your Kubernetes cluster and the management CLI tool. In this book, I will be using minikube, but you can use just about any Kubernetes cluster that you have access to.

Finally, you've installed Tekton—the CLI and the dashboard. Those are the tools you will use in the next chapters to create your CI/CD pipelines.

You are now ready to get started with Tekton, and in the next chapter, you will see how to use the most fundamental building block available to you: **Tasks**.

4
Stepping into Tasks

In the previous chapter, you prepared your local environment to build, manage, and run Tekton CI/CD pipelines. It is now time to get started with some hands-on examples. First, we will recap the concepts of Tasks from *Chapter 2, A Cloud-Native Approach to CI/CD*, and we will see where they fit in the context of Tekton Pipelines. We will then look at how to build your tasks. Getting a good understanding of the basic principles is key to mastering larger and more complex pipelines.

Once those have been covered, we will jump into some practical use cases. Starting with the most basic task possible, we will build on it to create something that can be used in your day-to-day life as a software developer. Once tasks have been executed, it will be possible to explore task runs and see those tasks' output. Apart from looking at the raw output, we will also explore ways to view that output with some of the tools you installed in the previous chapter.

After that, you will see how to make your tasks reusable with the addition of parameters and see how you can share information across Steps using shared volumes and results. Finally, you will learn some tricks on how to debug containers that are not working as expected. By then, you should be able to get started writing some tasks on your own. In the last section, you will have some exercises with the matching solutions that you can try on your own to sharpen your task writing skills.

In this chapter, we are going to cover the following main topics:

- Introducing tasks
- Understanding steps
- Building your first task
- Adding task parameters
- Sharing data
- Visualizing tasks
- Digging into TaskRuns
- Getting your hands dirty

Technical requirements

You can find all of the examples described in this chapter in the `chapter-4` folder of the Git repository: `https://github.com/PacktPublishing/Building-CI-CD-systems-using-Tekton`.

Check out the following link to see the Code in Action video: `https://bit.ly/3BKJxXM`

Introducing tasks

The first Tekton concept to which you will be introduced here is a task. Tasks are the basic building block that you will use to build your larger pipelines.

In a nutshell, tasks should perform a single operation in your CI/CD pipeline. Examples of tasks could include cloning a repository, compiling some code, or running a series of tests. Those tasks can take multiple forms and can be more or less complex, depending on your needs. When building your own, you should also try to make them as reusable as possible.

Tasks are defined with YAML files that describe what you want to achieve. The definition of a task follows the standard for all Kubernetes objects. You will specify the API version to use and the kind of object you are defining. Then add some metadata to identify the task.

As a rule of thumb, your tasks will always start like this:

```
apiVersion: tekton.dev/v1beta1
kind: Task
```

```
metadata:
  name: example-task-name
  labels:
    key: value
spec:
```

In the spec section, you will describe your actual task. This is where you will be defining the various elements you want to use to achieve the task's goal. Those elements could be parameters, workspaces, results, or steps.

Tasks are scoped to a single namespace in your cluster, but you might have **ClusterTasks** defined for the entire cluster by your administrators.

Once you trigger this task, everything will run inside a single Pod, which will be terminated once a step fails or once all of the steps are executed successfully. In the next section, you will see how you can use those steps to create your tasks.

Understanding Steps

Steps are the only required objects to create a task, and that makes sense. Steps describe the containers that will run as part of the task. This is where the actual operations to be performed on your inputs happen.

In the YAML file that describes the task, you define steps by adding an array describing the steps and the order they should be performed in.

Each step must have, at a minimum, an image to use. It is also highly recommended to use a command value or a script field. This is because the container's entry point is overwritten with an executable that manages the step execution for Tekton.

A typical Step would also contain a name and would generally look like this:

```
spec:
  steps:
    - image: alpine:3.12
      command:
        - /bin/bash
        - -c
        - echo Text from a step
```

If you want to use an image from a private registry, you can add an **ImagePullSecret** Kubernetes object to the service account used by the task. You will learn more on this topic in *Chapter 9, Securing Authentication*.

Now that you understand how tasks and Steps are defined, you will see how to use this knowledge to build your first working task.

Building your first task

In this section, you will create your first Hello World task. While this task might not be instrumental in your day-to-day life, it will demonstrate the basic concepts to build your first Tekton task:

1. First, start with a new YAML file called `hello.yaml`. In that file, start by specifying the API version to use and the kind of object described:

    ```
    apiVersion: tekton.dev/v1beta1
    kind: Task
    ```

2. Next, add in some metadata. For this first example, we will stick with the bare minimum and only add a task name:

    ```
    metadata:
      name: hello
    ```

3. Now that you've described the task and named it, you can add a spec for it. Here, it will contain a single step:

    ```
    spec:
      steps:
    ```

    For this single step, you will use the **Universal Base Images UBI** image to run a Bash script.

    > **About the UBI**
    >
    > Red Hat UBI offers a lightweight version of Red Hat Enterprise Linux as a base image to build your containers. It offers great reliability and high security for your containers to build on.

4. The Bash script that will be executed will have a single command, which will output "Hello World" to the standard output:

```
- image: registry.access.redhat.com/ubi8/ubi-minimal
  command:
    - /bin/bash
    - -c
    - echo "Hello World"
```

5. The full task, described here, can also be found in this book's GitHub repository under the name hello.yaml:

```
apiVersion: tekton.dev/v1beta1
kind: Task
metadata:
  name: hello
spec:
  steps:
    - image: registry.access.redhat.com/ubi8/ubi-minimal
      command:
        - /bin/bash
        - -c
        - echo "Hello World"
```

6. Now that you have your first task defined, you can apply it to your cluster using the kubectl tool in your terminal:

```
$ kubectl apply -f ./hello.yaml
```

7. It is now time to use the tkn CLI tool to manage and execute this task. All the commands that are related to tasks can be used with the task subcommand. You can list the tasks that are available in the cluster by using ls, as shown here:

```
$ tkn task ls
NAME      DESCRIPTION    AGE
hello                    2 minutes ago
```

8. You should see the task that you've just created here. Now that you know this task is available for you to use, you can start it by using the start command followed by the task's name:

```
$ tkn task start hello
TaskRun started: hello-run-j4q46


In order to track the TaskRun progress run:
tkn taskrun logs hello-run-j4q46 -f -n default
```

Notice that this created a TaskRun with a random name. The TaskRun, which is the actual execution of this task, is now running in your cluster. Because this task is running inside a Pod on the cluster, you can't see the logs directly in your console. You can use the command stated by the CLI tool to view the logs, or you can use the --showlog argument when you start the task to view the logs directly.

9. Try starting this task with the --showlog argument to see the output from the step:

```
$ tkn task start hello --showlog
TaskRun started: hello-run-zf5hh
Waiting for logs to be available...


[unnamed-0] Hello World
```

This started a new task run with a new random name. This time, you will see the outputs of each step as they are executed. The outputs will be prefixed with the name of the step from which the log originates. In this case, since you did not name the step, Tekton automatically named it unnamed-0.

Adding additional Steps

In many cases, your tasks will have more than one step. This is why the steps field is a list. You can specify multiple steps using various images. The following is how you build such a task:

1. Start by creating a new file called multiple.yaml and start with the basic task definition:

```
apiVersion: tekton.dev/v1beta1
kind: Task
metadata:
```

```
  name: multiple-steps
spec:
  steps:
```

2. For the first step, you can use a UBI and echo a statement. This time, you should give a name to your step to differentiate it for when you look at the log outputs:

```
  - name: first
    image: registry.access.redhat.com/ubi8/ubi-minimal
    command:
      - /bin/bash
      - -c
      - echo "First step running"
```

For the second task, you can use a different image if you are so inclined. In this case, you can use an Alpine image, which is another lightweight Linux base image. This image does not have the Bash shell, but you can use sh instead.

3. Use an echo statement to show some output in the logs similar to what was done for the first step:

```
  - name: second
    image: alpine
    command:
      - /bin/sh
      - -c
      - echo "Second step running"
```

4. The final file can be found in the repository as multiple.yaml and should look like this:

```
apiVersion: tekton.dev/v1beta1
kind: Task
metadata:
  name: multiple-steps
spec:
  steps:
    - name: first
      image: registry.access.redhat.com/ubi8/ubi-minimal
      command:
```

```
          - /bin/bash
          - -c
          - echo "First step running"
  - name: second
    image: alpine
    command:
          - /bin/sh
          - -c
          - echo "Second step running"
```

5. You are now ready to apply this task to your cluster and look at the task's output with multiple steps. Just like you did for your first task, you can use the `kubectl` command to create this task:

```
$ kubectl apply -f ./multiple.yaml
```

Now that the task is created, you should see it when you run the `ls` subcommand to view the available tasks:

```
$ tkn task ls
NAME                 DESCRIPTION       AGE
hello                                  57 minutes ago
multiple-steps                         8 minutes ago
```

6. Go ahead and run this task to see the outputs of each `echo` statement:

```
$ tkn task start multiple-steps --showlog
TaskRun started: multiple-steps-run-cvgwm
Waiting for logs to be available...


[first] First step running


[second] Second step running
```

The log prefix is color-coded to make it easier to distinguish between the various steps. If you have a terminal that does not support **ANSI color codes**, you can disable this feature with the `--no-color` argument:

```
$ tkn task start multiple-steps --showlog --no-color
```

Apart from the colors, now using your terminal defaults, the results should be the same.

Using scripts

Sometimes, you will want to perform an operation that is more complex in your steps' command field. To do so, you can use a script instead of the command you used previously. These two are mutually exclusive. You can only have a single command or a single script, but not both.

To do so, start with a new YAML file called `script.yaml`. To that file, add the standard task definition and name the task `script`. In the `spec` section, add a single step as follows. This time, you will install an additional package to be used by the UBI, so you will need to use the `ubi` variant instead of the `ubi-minimal` variant used previously:

```
    - name: step-with-script
      image: registry.access.redhat.com/ubi8/ubi
      script: |
        #!/usr/bin/env bash
        echo "Installing necessary tooling"
        dnf install iputils -y
        ping redhat.com -c 5
        echo "All done!"
```

Here, instead of using a command, a script is used, followed by a pipe (|) symbol. All of the lines at the same indentation level are then executed as part of the script. In this case, this is a Bash script that starts with an `echo` statement. It then installs the `iputils` package. Once installed, it can use the `ping` command to check the latency with a website. Finally, it echoes `"All done!"`.

The final file can be found in the repository under the name `script.yaml` and should look like this:

```
apiVersion: tekton.dev/v1beta1
kind: Task
metadata:
  name: script
spec:
  steps:
    - name: step-with-script
      image: registry.access.redhat.com/ubi8/ubi
      script: |
        #!/usr/bin/env bash
        echo "Installing necessary tooling"
```

```
        dnf install iputils -y
        ping redhat.com -c 5
        echo "All done!"
```

You can then apply this task to your cluster and run it with the Tekton CLI tool to see the output:

```
$ kubectl apply -f ./script.yaml
task.tekton.dev/script created

$ tkn task start script --showlog
TaskRun started: script-run-4zdlh
Waiting for logs to be available...
[step-with-script] Installing necessary tooling
...
[step-with-script] Installed:
[step-with-script]    iputils-20180629-2.el8.x86_64
...
[step-with-script] 64 bytes from redirect.redhat.com
(209.132.183.105): icmp_seq=3 ttl=234 time=80.10 ms
...
[step-with-script] All done!
```

> **Note**
>
> Some of the logs' lines have been redacted for readability; your output should be much longer.

The script's first line used a shebang (#!) to tell the operating system which interpreter to use to parse the script that followed. In the previous example, Bash was used. If you have an image with other executables, you could also use those to run the script. For example, this step example uses a node image, and the script, written in JavaScript, is parsed by the node executable:

```
- image: node:14
  script: |
    #!/usr/bin/env node
    console.log("This is some JS code");
```

You now know how to create tasks to be used in Tekton. You can write a new task each time you need to perform an action in your CI/CD pipelines, but ideally, you will want to reuse as much as possible across all of your pipelines. This is part of Tekton's main objectives: to make reusable components. To help make your tasks more versatile, you will need to use parameters.

Adding task parameters

One of the goals that you should aim for when building your tasks is to make them as reusable as possible. A simple way to reuse a task in different contexts is to add parameters to them. You can then substitute the values of those parameters in the steps that compose your task.

Making the Hello task more reusable

For this first example, you can create a new file called `hello-param.yaml` in which you will copy the content of the existing `hello.yaml` file.

The goal is now to make this task reusable in different contexts. Instead of simply always outputting Hello World, we now want it to say hello to anyone, not just the world.

Parameters are added in the `spec` section of the task. This new `params` field will contain a list of parameters. For each parameter, you will add a name and a type. The type can be either `string` or `array`.

In this case, there will be a single parameter named who, and it will be of type `string`:

```
params:
  - name: who
    type: string
```

Next, you will want to use variable substitution to extract the value of that parameter. In any fields of the steps, you can use `$(params.<NAME_OF_PARAMETER>)`. This will be replaced with the value of the given parameter.

In the case of this hello task, you can change the word "World" in the last element of the `command` array to `$(params.who)`:

```
command:
  - /bin/bash
  - -c
  - echo "Hello $(params.who)"
```

Don't forget to change your task's name if you don't want to overwrite the original hello task. Your final `hello-param.yaml` file should now look like this:

```yaml
apiVersion: tekton.dev/v1beta1
kind: Task
metadata:
  name: hello-param
spec:
  params:
    - name: who
      type: string
  steps:
    - image: registry.access.redhat.com/ubi8/ubi-minimal
      command:
        - /bin/bash
        - -c
        - echo "Hello $(params.who)"
```

You are now ready to run your first parametrized task. Start this new task just as you would with any other normal task:

```
$ tkn task start hello-param --showlog
? Value for param `who` of type `string`? Joel
TaskRun started: hello-param-run-sfzv7
Waiting for logs to be available...

[unnamed-0] Hello Joel
```

This time, you should be prompted by the `tkn` CLI tool to add a value for the `who` parameter. You can also pass in the values for the parameters directly in the command line by using the -p argument:

```
$ tkn task start hello-param --showlog -p who=Joel
```

The result will be the same, but Tekton won't prompt you for the parameter value.

Using array type parameters

You can also use parameters of type array. These parameters will contain an array of values that can then be expanded anywhere an array is used. This type of parameter can be convenient when you expect an unknown number of arguments to a command or a script that you might want to run.

In this next example, you will create a task that can take any number of grocery items and then list them in the form of a grocery list.

Start by creating a new file named groceries.yaml in which you will add the template for a task called groceries. Then, in spec, add a parameter named grocery-items of type array:

```
params:
  - name: grocery-items
    type: array
```

Now create a step that will use the node:14 base image. Name this step grocery-list. Then add a Node.js script that will take any arguments and then log them to the standard output. Finally, you can add the args property, which will expand the grocery-item parameter using the star (*) operator:

```
- name: grocery-list
  image: node:14
  args:
    - $(params.grocery-items[*])
  script: |
    #!/usr/bin/env node
    const items = process.argv.splice(2);
    console.log("Grocery List");
    items.map(i => console.log(`=> ${i}`));
```

When you run this task, you will be asked to enter a value for grocery-items. You can type in a list of comma-separated values here. Try typing in "milk,bread,apples":

```
$ kubectl apply -f ./groceries.yaml
task.tekton.dev/groceries created


$ tkn task start groceries --showlog
? Value for param `grocery-items` of type `array`?
milk,bread,apples
```

```
TaskRun started: groceries-run-k7dtk
Waiting for logs to be available...

[grocery-list] Grocery List
[grocery-list] => milk
[grocery-list] => bread
[grocery-list] => apples
```

This would be the same result as if you had written your task with the following hard-coded values:

```
args:
   - milk
   - bread
   - apples
```

A more common use case for this type of parameter would be a step that uses a CLI tool, and you want to give the user the option to add extra parameters or flags to the command.

For example, if you had a step that used a `curl` command, you could add an array parameter to take various flags and a string parameter for the URL. This way, if the user wants to pass in an extra header, they will have the ability to do so.

Adding a default value

You can also add a default value to your parameters. You can do this by adding a default field to the `param` object. Try changing your `hello-param.yaml` file to add a default value to the parameter named `who`:

```
   - name: who
     type: string
     default: World
```

Don't forget to apply this new file to your Kubernetes cluster:

```
$ kubectl apply -f ./hello-param-defaults.yaml
task.tekton.dev/hello-param configured
```

The next time you start this task, you will see the default value proposed by the `tkn` CLI tool. Hit *Enter* to accept the default value suggested:

```
$ tkn task start hello-param --showlog
```

```
? Value for param `who` of type `string`? (Default is `World`)
World
TaskRun started: hello-param-run-vw75m
Waiting for logs to be available...

[unnamed-0] Hello World
```

You can also use `--use-param-defaults` to start this task run immediately with the default values for those parameters:

```
$ tkn task start hello-param --showlog --use-param-defaults
TaskRun started: hello-param-run-tgfwx
Waiting for logs to be available...

[unnamed-0] Hello World
```

Task parameters can be used in one or many steps if you need to. That can be useful to share inputs for your steps, but if you need to bring over the output of a step into a subsequent step, that won't work. Thankfully, there are ways to share information across steps using shared volumes.

Sharing data

Because all the steps in a task are actually containers running in a single Pod, it is possible to share volumes across those containers. In fact, tasks already do that for you. There are various ways to use this volume, or you could mount your own from an existing **PersistentVolumeClaim**.

Accessing the home directory

> **Deprecation notice**
>
> As documented in pull request #3878 (`https://github.com/tektoncd/pipeline/pull/3878`), this feature has been deprecated as of version 0.24. If you are using version 0.20.1 as specified in *Chapter 3, Installation and Getting Started*, it might work, but there are no guarantees that it won't break when using a more recent version of Tekton.

An easy way to share information across your steps is to use the home directory directly. When tasks are initiated, the task run will mount a volume named /tekton/home in each container that runs a step. Accessing this folder is simply a matter of changing the directory to ~.

To see how you can do this, you can create a new task called shared-home:

```
apiVersion: tekton.dev/v1beta1
kind: Task
metadata:
  name: shared-home
spec:
  steps:
```

In the spec section, you will add two steps. The first step, named write, will use the minimal UBI8 image. It will use a script to perform the following operations.

First, it will go to the home folder. Next, it will echo a statement so that you have a log output. It will also specify the full path to the current folder to see where the home folder is located. Finally, it will write a secret message to a file called message.txt:

```
  - name: write
    image: registry.access.redhat.com/ubi8/ubi-minimal
    script: |
      cd ~
      echo "Getting ready to write to" $(pwd)
      echo "Secret Message" > message.txt
```

The second step will use the same UBI image to list the ~/message.txt file using the cat CLI tool:

```
  - name: read
    image: registry.access.redhat.com/ubi8/ubi-minimal
    command:
      - /bin/bash
    args: ["-c", "cat ~/message.txt"]
```

You can apply this file and run the task called `shared-home`. You should see the write step showing that it is getting ready to write to `/tekton/home`, and then the read step will output the secret message:

```
$ kubectl apply -f ./shared-home.yaml
task.tekton.dev/shared-home created

$ tkn task start shared-home --showlog
TaskRun started: shared-home-run-gtllf
Waiting for logs to be available...

[write] Getting ready to write to /tekton/home

[read] Secret Message
```

Accessing the `home` folder directly is an easy way to carry information across containers, but there is no guarantee that the Tekton team will keep this way of doing things. There is a more official way to share information, and that is called **results**.

Using results

Results can be used in tasks to store the output from a task in a single file. Ultimately, the result is the same as using the `home` folder directly, but it is a standard way of sharing limited pieces of data across steps or even between tasks. If you are looking to share larger pieces of data, this will be addressed in *Chapter 7, Sharing Data with Workspaces*.

Results are added to the task `spec` and will have a name and a description. Those results will then map to files stored in the `/tekton/results` folder. To access the result, you can use variable extrapolation to get the path of the file.

To try this out, follow these steps:

1. Create a new task named `results` and add a result as part of `spec`. This result will be named `message` and have a description:

```
apiVersion: tekton.dev/v1beta1
kind: Task
metadata:
  name: using-results
spec:
  results:
```

```
    - name: message
      description: Message to be shared
  steps:
```

2. Next, you can use the UBI image to create a `base64` encoded string and store that message into the result for your write step. You can get the path name by extrapolating `$(results.<result_name>.path)`:

```
  - name: write
    image: registry.access.redhat.com/ubi8/ubi-minimal
    command:
      - /bin/bash
    args:
      - "-c"
      - echo "Secret Message" | base64 > $(results.
message.path)
```

3. You can use the same variable to access this file in the read step and output the file's content:

```
  - name: read
    image: registry.access.redhat.com/ubi8/ubi-minimal
    command:
      - /bin/bash
    args:
      - "-c"
      - cat $(results.message.path)
```

4. If you apply this file to your cluster and run this task, you should see the secret message being displayed in the read step logs:

```
$ kubectl apply -f ./results.yaml
task.tekton.dev/using-results created

$ tkn task start using-results --showlog
TaskRun started: using-results-run-qmkcg
Waiting for logs to be available...

[read] U2VjcmV0IE1lc3NhZ2UK
```

The maximum size of a result is 4,096 bytes. This is due to the container termination message feature of Kubernetes used by Tekton to create those results.

Using results can be useful for passing small bits of information across various steps. If you need to share larger objects, you might need to resort to more classic volumes in Kubernetes.

Using Kubernetes volumes

Just like with any other Kubernetes Pods, you can mount a volume into your tasks so that it can share data between the containers running in it or with other parts of the system. As an example, you could store some configuration settings as part of a **ConfigMap** and then mount it as a volume so you can access it from your tasks.

A ConfigMap is a Kubernetes resource that allows you to store non-encrypted data as key-value pairs.

In this next example, you will create a ConfigMap containing color codes to be used by the `echo` statements. In a file called `configmap.yaml`, start with the following ConfigMap:

```
apiVersion: v1
kind: ConfigMap
metadata:
  name: colors-map
data:
  error: "\e[31m"
  info: "\e[34m"
  debug: "\e[32m"
```

This will create three files called `error`, `info`, and `debug`. The files' content is the ANSI code that will be used to colorize the `echo` statements in the task. This could be useful if you wanted to use a different color scheme between various systems or if you wanted to standardize it across all your tasks.

Next, create a new task called `configmap`:

```
apiVersion: tekton.dev/v1beta1
kind: Task
metadata:
  name: configmap
spec:
```

You can start by adding a volume that will use the ConfigMap you just created in `spec`:

```
volumes:
  - name: colors
    configMap:
      name: colors-map
```

This will let you mount this volume as part of a step. The step you will create here will use a UBI container to echo three statements. Each statement uses the content of the files from the mounted volume to add a color code:

```
steps:
  - name: log-stuff
    image: registry.access.redhat.com/ubi8/ubi-minimal
    volumeMounts:
      - name: colors
        mountPath: /var/colors
    script: |
      echo $(cat /var/colors/info)Logging information
      echo $(cat /var/colors/debug)Debugging statement
      echo $(cat /var/colors/error)Colorized error
```

You are now ready to apply this file and run this task. The output will have the colors blue, green, and red.

Note that ConfigMaps are mounted as a read-only filesystem and can't be used to store information within the pods.

This example used a ConfigMap, but you could also use a `Secret` or a `PersistentVolumeClaim` here, although the Tekton way to do this would be using a `workspace`.

Using workspaces

You can use workspaces to mount different types of volumes to be shared across steps in a task or across tasks in a pipeline, depending on your use case. Workspaces can provide you with an interface that works better with your Tekton pipelines. For this reason, they have an entire chapter dedicated to them in this book (*Chapter 7, Sharing Data with Workspaces*).

Now that you have a few tasks that have run in your cluster, you will need a way to see whether they ran successfully and understand what happened if they didn't.

Visualizing tasks

So far, you've used the `tkn` CLI tool to visualize the tasks that you have added to your cluster, but that is not the only way. If you've installed the **Visual Studio Code** (**VS Code**) extension and Tekton Dashboard, you can find more information about your tasks there.

The VS Code Tekton Pipelines extension

If you installed the Tekton Pipelines VS Code extension in *Chapter 3*, *Installation and Getting Started*, then you have access to the Tekton pipelines panel directly from your IDE. If you select the Tekton pipelines in the navigation bar, it should open up a panel that describes everything related to Tekton that you have on this cluster.

You can see that panel in the following screenshot:

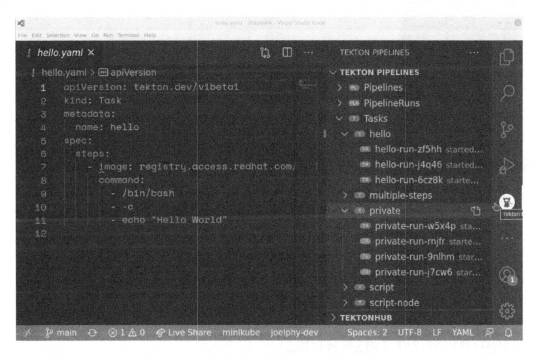

Figure 4.1 – The Tekton Pipelines panel in VS Code

From this view, you can see the list of tasks that you've created already. If you click on one of them, you will also see all the associated task runs and their state.

This view can be useful to see which of your tasks were executed successfully and which failed. You can also find out more information about the task runs and see each step's status there.

Tekton Dashboard

If you installed Tekton Dashboard in *Chapter 3, Installation and Getting Started*, you can use it to visualize the tasks that you have created so far and the associated task runs, as shown in the following screenshot:

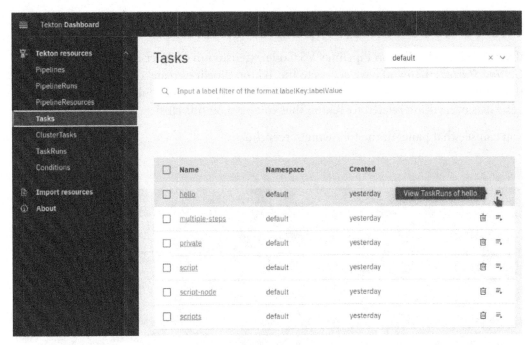

Figure 4.2 – Tekton Dashboard in action

Tekton Dashboard provides you with a clean UI to look at everything associated with Tekton currently available in your cluster. If you click on the **View TaskRuns** button, you will see all the executions of this task. If you select one of those task runs, you will see the status of each step along with all the logs. This can help you understand what is happening if you have a task that does not give you the expected output.

Digging into TaskRuns

Task runs are the actual executions of the tasks themselves. Tasks are essentially just a template to build task runs. When you use the `tkn` CLI tool to start a task, it uses that template, binds the parameters and the options, and then starts the execution.

The visualization tools, such as the VS Code extension or Tekton Dashboard, can help get some insights about the task runs, but sometimes, you might need more information.

To see the content of a task run, start by creating one for the `groceries` Task that you created earlier:

```
$ tkn task start groceries --showlog
? Value for param `grocery-items` of type `array`?
milk,bread,coffee
TaskRun started: groceries-run-k24zp
Waiting for logs to be available...

[grocery-list] Grocery List
[grocery-list] => milk
[grocery-list] => bread
[grocery-list] => coffee
```

Notice the line that starts with `TaskRun started`. It should show the name of the task run that was just started. This is a random name, so those last five characters might differ when you run it.

To see the content of that task run, you will use `kubectl`:

```
$ kubectl get taskrun groceries-run-k24zp -o yaml
```

This will output the YAML description of the task run to your standard output. There is a lot of content in that file. A lot of it is metadata, which we can ignore for now. If you look at the `params` section, you will see the `params` object here, filled with the data that you entered in the CLI:

```
params:
- name: grocery-items
  value:
  - milk
  - bread
  - coffee
```

When Tekton creates the task run, it fills in those values from the CLI tool to create this object. The same process is applied when mounting volumes or anything else through the `tkn` tool.

If you scroll down a little bit, you will also find a `status` object:

```
status:
  completionTime: "2021-02-26T21:12:51Z"
```

```yaml
  conditions:
  - lastTransitionTime: "2021-02-26T21:12:51Z"
    message: All Steps have completed executing
    reason: Succeeded
    status: "True"
    type: Succeeded
  podName: groceries-run-k24zp-pod-xfrrl
  startTime: "2021-02-26T21:12:44Z"
```

Here, you can find all the information about the status of this task. In this case, the task succeeded, and you can see when it started and when it ended.

This `status` object also contains a `steps` object:

```yaml
  steps:
  - container: step-grocery-list
    imageID: docker-pullable://node@
sha256:1b1bf1f5023ddd7e08774fa5fcef15f3773833b194bac4e55134fa5
f156dcdd6
    name: grocery-list
    terminated:
      containerID:
docker://637e04088c6af1bfcc52b0d8d32d43858e9a
ed1d7f9b709804e43fd78de57514
      exitCode: 0
      finishedAt: "2021-02-26T21:12:50Z"
      reason: Completed
      startedAt: "2021-02-26T21:12:50Z"
```

This section of the YAML file will provide you with the status of each step from your task. You can see the container that was used along with start and finish timestamps. You also have the exit code and the reason for the container termination.

These outputs can be handy if you need to understand why a task did not successfully complete. You can look at each step and try to understand what happened. As an example, create the following task in a file named `failing.yaml`:

```yaml
apiVersion: tekton.dev/v1beta1
kind: Task
metadata:
```

```
    name: failing
spec:
  steps:
    - image: nonexistinguser/notavalidcontainer
      command:
        - echo "Hello World"
```

Start this task and then get the content of the task run that was created:

```
$ kubectl apply -f ./failing.yaml
task.tekton.dev/failing created
```

```
$ tkn task start failing
TaskRun started: failing-run-grxqv
```

Notice how the --showlog parameter was intentionally not used here. If you accidentally typed it in, you would see that the task execution is halted. You can use *Ctrl + C* to stop watching for the logs.

Now this task failed without providing you with an error message. You can inspect the task run to have an understanding of what happened:

```
$ kubectl get tr failing-run-grxqv -o yaml
```

If you scroll down to the steps section, you will see the following for the unnamed-0 step:

```
    - container: step-unnamed-0
      name: unnamed-0
      waiting:
        message: Back-off pulling image "nonexistinguser/
notavalidcontainer"
        reason: ImagePullBackOff
```

You can see that the problem is that the image nonexistinguser/notavalidcontainer does not exist and can't be pulled from the registry.

Now that you know how to debug your failing tasks, it is time for you to try building your own task.

Getting your hands dirty

It is time for you to test out those newly learned skills. You can find a solution to those problems in the *Assessments* section of this book. Those challenges will use the concepts that you have seen in this chapter.

More than Hello World

In this first challenge, build a task with three steps. The first step should output a log message stating that the task has started. Then, the task will sleep for a number of seconds that the user specifies. In the third step, the task should log a string that the user provides. Be sure to add default values to those two parameters. Now try running the task with the `tkn` CLI tool. Run it a second time using the default values this time. Start this task a third time, specifying the parameter values directly in the command line.

> **Tips**
>
> - You will have three steps and two parameters in this task.
>
> - Use the default field to set a default value to the parameters.
>
> - With the CLI tool, you can use the `--use-default-params` and `-p` flags to specify the parameter values.

Build a generic curl task

For this challenge, build a task that will use the `curl` application to fetch some information about a web page. The user should pass in any argument that can be used with `curl` along with the URL to reach. The output of `curl` should be produced in a separate task.

> **Tips**
>
> - You will need two parameters and two steps for this task.
>
> - Using an `array` parameter will let you accept multiple arguments.
>
> - The first step should produce a result that the second step can pick up.

Create a random user

For this challenge, create a task that will make a request to the Random User API (`http://randomuser.me`) and extract the first and last name of the random user that was generated. The `nat` parameter to specify the randomly generated user's nationality should be specified in a ConfigMap.

> **Tips:**
>
> - You can use the URL `https://randomuser.me/api/?inc=name,nat&nat=<nationality>` to generate a user, where `<nationality>` should be one of AU, BR, CA, CH, DE, DK, ES, FI, FR, GB, IE, IR, NO, NL, NZ, TR, and US.
>
> - `curl` can take a configuration file that has the value for the URL.
>
> - Try using three steps: one to generate the configuration file, one to do a `curl`, and one to extract the data.
>
> - An image called `stedolan/jq` provides you with the `jq` tool to extract data from a JSON file.

Summary

Now you know everything there is to know about tasks. Throughout this chapter, you've learned more about how tasks and Steps relate to each other. You've also seen how each task runs in a single Pod and how the steps each run in their own containers.

This chapter also showed you how to build your first tasks. You can now build a Tekton task that contains multiple steps along with a collection of parameters. For when you want to share data between those containers running in the task, you have learned about different ways to do so.

Finally, you have also seen how to debug your containers by using some visualization tools, such as the Tekton VS Code extension and Tekton Dashboard. If you need more details, you also know how to analyze the content of a task run.

Understanding how to create those basic building blocks is key to building efficient Tekton CI/CD pipelines, and now that you have this knowledge, you are ready to jump into pipelines in the next chapter.

5
Jumping into Pipelines

So far, you've seen how to install and use Tekton in your Kubernetes cluster. You've also explored how tasks work and how you can use them to perform various operations inside a pod. Tasks can do some powerful stuff on their own, but they are still somewhat limited. What happens if you want to perform more than one operation? This is where pipelines will come into play. In this chapter, you will learn everything there is to know about pipelines.

First, you will learn a little more about pipelines and where they fit in your CI/CD processes. Once you understand what they are and how they work, you will be introduced to some hands-on examples.

Similar to what was done in the last chapter, you will start by creating a simple `Hello-World` pipeline to get you accustomed to the general syntax.

Then, we will introduce some more advanced concepts. You will see how to use parameters to make your pipelines more versatile and ensure that your tasks are happening in the order you expect them to.

Next, you will also see how you can reuse some tasks in the context of a single pipeline by using those parameters.

Once those principles have been covered, you will be able to build your own pipelines. Still, before you jump into some exercises, you will see how you can visualize pipelines and pipeline runs to help you debug them if they fail to run as expected.

In this chapter, we are going to cover the following main topics:

- Introducing pipelines
- Building your first pipeline
- Parameterizing pipelines
- Reusing tasks in the context of a pipeline
- Ordering tasks within pipelines
- Using task results in pipelines
- Introducing pipeline runs
- Getting your hands dirty

Technical requirements

You can find all of the examples described in this chapter in the `chapter-5` folder of the Git repository: `https://github.com/PacktPublishing/Building-CI-CD-systems-using-Tekton`.

You can also see the code in action videos at `https://bit.ly/3zCNbkk`.

Introducing pipelines

Now that you have a better understanding of steps and tasks, it's time to introduce pipelines. Pipelines are a collection of tasks that are designed to produce an output from your inputs.

While a task is in charge of a single operation inside your CI/CD pipeline, a pipeline will use those tasks to perform the desired automation processes on your source code. For example, a pipeline could use a task to clone a code repository and a second task to run unit tests, and finally, have one last task to build an image ready to be deployed on your production servers.

Just like with tasks, you should aim at making your pipelines as reusable as possible. There is a good chance that most of your projects that use a similar tech stack will use the same pipeline, the only difference being the initial code repository and image name that is produced.

Pipelines use YAML files to describe the processes that will occur and the order in which those operations need to happen. They also follow the same syntax that any Kubernetes object would.

A typical pipeline starts with the following YAML description:

```yaml
apiVersion: tekton.dev/v1beta1
kind: Pipeline
metadata:
name: example-pipeline
labels:
   key: value
spec:
```

The bulk of the pipeline is then described in the `spec` object. The only required option in `spec` is the `task` list to describe the pods that should run as part of this CI/CD pipeline.

Just like tasks create task runs when started, pipelines will generate pipeline runs, which are the actual executions of a pipeline. In that sense, you can consider a pipeline as a template for your pipeline runs.

You can now get started and create your first pipeline.

Building your first pipeline

For this first pipeline, you will create a task that will output some text, similar to the `hello world` task used in the last chapter. You will then use this task to build your first pipeline:

1. First, start with your basic `task` object in a file called `hello-pipeline.yaml`:

    ```yaml
    apiVersion: tekton.dev/v1beta1
    kind: Task
    metadata:
      name: first-task
    spec:
      steps:
    ```

2. By now, you know that you can create a simple step that produces an `echo` statement using a UBI container. You can keep this step with the minimal information necessary to run:

```
- image: registry.access.redhat.com/ubi8/ubi-minimal
  command:
    - /bin/bash
  args: ['-c', 'echo Hello from first task']
```

> **Note**
>
> You can add multiple Tekton objects in a YAML file using the `- - -` separator in your file.

3. You can now add the pipeline base definition in this same file:

```
apiVersion: tekton.dev/v1beta1
kind: Pipeline
metadata:
  name: hello
spec:
```

4. The `spec` section will require a list of tasks that will be executed as part of this pipeline. Create that list and add your first task. Contrary to steps, tasks must have a name. Give the name `first` to this task. The other required field is the task reference. There, you specify the task to be used, that is, the task called `first-task` that you just created:

```
tasks:
  - name: first
    taskRef:
      name: first-task
```

That is the most basic pipeline that you can create. It has a single task running a single step.

5. You can apply this file to your Kubernetes cluster with the `kubectl` CLI, just like you did for tasks:

```
$ kubectl apply -f ./hello-pipeline.yaml
task.tekton.dev/first-task created
pipeline.tekton.dev/hello created
```

6. To create a pipeline run based on this pipeline, you can use the `tkn` CLI tool. The syntax is almost identical to when you used it for managing tasks. To start this pipeline, you can use `tkn` with the `pipeline` subcommand. Then, use the `start` argument followed by the name of the pipeline to start it:

```
$ tkn pipeline start hello
PipelineRun started: hello-run-bf6h5

In order to track the PipelineRun progress run:
tkn pipelinerun logs hello-run-bf6h5 -f -n default
```

7. You can use the same flags that you used for your tasks. For example, to see the logs directly, you can use the `--showlog` flag:

```
$ tkn pipeline start hello --showlog
PipelineRun started: hello-run-6nzm6
Waiting for logs to be available...
[first : unnamed-0] Hello from first task
```

There it is, you have built and executed your first Tekton pipeline. So far, the output is very similar to what happened when you started your first tasks. The difference here is that the pipeline is the one that initiated the tasks. Also, note how the prefix to the logs now has two values separated by a colon. Instead of simply outputting the step name, as it did previously, the output now has the name of the task, followed by the step's name. This makes it easier to see exactly what is happening during the execution of this pipeline. You can see an example of those logs when you add a new task to your pipeline:

1. Create a new task in a file named `die-roll.yaml`. This file will contain the definition for a task named `die-roll`:

```
apiVersion: tekton.dev/v1beta1
kind: Task
metadata:
  name: die-roll
spec:
  steps:
```

To see what the output looks like with multiple steps, this task will have two steps. The first step will output a greeting message, and the second step will output a random number between 1 and 6.

2. The first step, called `greeting`, uses a UBI and issues an `echo` statement that says `Rolling 6-sided dice`:

```
- name: greetings
  image: registry.access.redhat.com/ubi8/ubi-minimal
  command:
  - /bin/bash
  args: ['-c', 'echo Rolling 6-sided dice']
```

3. The second step, named `generate-random-number`, will use a node image, and a script will be executed to generate a random number between 1 and 6:

```
- name: generating-random-number
  image: node:14
  script: |
    #!/usr/bin/env node
    const max = 6
    let randomNumber = Math.floor(Math.random() *
Math.floor(max));
    console.log(randomNumber + 1);
```

4. You can now add this new task to the `hello` pipeline. First, add the base definition for the pipeline in a new file called `hello-dice-roll.yaml`:

```
apiVersion: tekton.dev/v1beta1
kind: Pipeline
metadata:
  name: hello-dice-roll
spec:
  tasks:
```

5. Keep the first task identical to the one in the `hello` pipeline:

```
- name: first
  taskRef:
    name: first-task
```

6. Then, add a second task named `roll` that will reference the `die-roll` task:

```
- name: roll
  taskRef:
    name: die-roll
```

7. Apply this file to your cluster and run this new pipeline to see the output:

```
$ kubectl apply -f ./hello-dice-roll.yaml
pipeline.tekton.dev/hello-dice-roll created

$ tkn pipeline start hello-dice-roll --showlog
PipelineRun started: hello-dice-roll-run-5rx4d
Waiting for logs to be available...
[first : unnamed-0] Hello from first task
[roll : greetings] Rolling Dice
[roll : generating-random-number] 4
```

You can now see how each log line is prefixed with the task's name, followed by the step's name. Assuming that you have a color terminal, you will also notice that each step name has a different color. When running multiple tasks with multiple steps, this can make it easier to distinguish where the logs come from and to spot an error in your CI/CD pipelines.

That works well for now, but what if you wanted to roll a 20-sided die the next time you start this pipeline? This is where adding parameters to your pipelines will come into play.

Parameterizing pipelines

Just like with tasks, you can add parameters to your Tekton pipelines. Those parameters would then typically be used as parameters for the tasks inside of them. By using parameters in your pipelines, you will reuse the same pipeline for multiple usages. For example, if you had a CI/CD pipeline to compile a Java application, you could reuse that pipeline across all of your projects, as long as the URL of the Git repository is a parameter.

In this next example, you will rewrite the tasks and pipeline from the last section, but this time keeping reusability in mind:

1. First, create a new file called `die-roll-param.yaml` and copy over the content from `die-roll.yaml`.

2. Next, add a parameter for the number of sides for the dice you want to roll. This parameter will be of the `string` type. You can also add a `default` value of `"6"`. This parameter takes a string as an argument, so don't forget the quotes around the `default` value:

```
- name: sides
  description: Number of sides to the dice
  default: "6"
  type: string
```

3. Now that you have a parameter, change the greetings step to use this new parameter in the `echo` statement. To use the parameter value, you can use the variable substitution shown here:

```
args: ['-c', 'echo Rolling $(params.sides)-sided
dice']
```

4. Similarly, use that variable substitution in the `generate-random-number` step to assign this value to the `max` variable in the Node.js script:

```
const max = $(params.sides)
```

Your new task should now look like this:

```
apiVersion: tekton.dev/v1beta1
kind: Task
metadata:
  name: die-roll-param
spec:
  params:
    - name: sides
      description: Number of sides to the dice
      default: "6"
      type: string
  steps:
    - name: greetings
      image: registry.access.redhat.com/ubi8/ubi-minimal
      command:
        - /bin/bash
      args: ['-c', 'echo Rolling $(params.sides)-sided
dice']
```

```
- name: generate-random-number
  image: node:14
  script: |
    #!/usr/bin/env node
    const max = $(params.sides)
    let randomNumber =  Math.floor(Math.random() *
Math.floor(max));
    console.log(randomNumber + 1);
```

Now that you have a task that will accept a parameter, you can use it in the context of a pipeline:

1. In a new file called `parametrized-dice-roll.yaml`, create a new `Pipeline` object:

```
apiVersion: tekton.dev/v1beta1
kind: Pipeline
metadata:
  name: parametrized-dice-roll
spec:
  tasks:
```

2. Add the first task exactly as you did before:

```
- name: first
  taskRef:
    name: first-task
```

3. Add a second task that will use the task you've just created:

```
- name: roll
  taskRef:
    name: die-roll-param
```

4. Apply those files and start the pipeline to see the output:

```
$ kubectl apply -f ./die-roll-param.yaml
task.tekton.dev/die-roll-param configured

$ kubectl apply -f ./parametrized-dice-roll.yaml
```

```
pipeline.tekton.dev/parametrized-dice-roll configured

$ tkn pipeline start parametrized-dice-roll --showlog
PipelineRun started: parametrized-dice-roll-run-1f7mh
Waiting for logs to be available...
[first : unnamed-0] Hello from first task
[roll : greetings] Rolling 6-sided dice
[roll : generate-random-number] 6
```

You will notice that the output is the same. This is because the pipeline used the default value from the task.

As part of the task definition, you can add a value for the task parameters. The task will then pick up this value, and you will see different outputs.

Using the same parametrized-dice-roll pipeline, change the definition of the task named roll to use a parameter called sides with the value 8:

```
- name: roll
  params:
    - name: sides
      value: "8"
  taskRef:
    name: die-roll-param
```

Now apply this file and rerun the pipeline:

```
$ kubectl apply -f ./parametrized-dice-roll-task-param.yaml
pipeline.tekton.dev/parametrized-dice-roll configured

$ tkn pipeline start parametrized-dice-roll --showlog
PipelineRun started: parametrized-dice-roll-run-m42m4
Waiting for logs to be available...
[first : unnamed-0] Hello from first task
[roll : greetings] Rolling 8-sided dice
[roll : generate-random-number] 7
```

This time, the dice roll was done with an 8-sided die, and the random number generated has a value between 1 and 8. Yet, this value is still hardcoded in the pipeline definition. Thankfully, there is a way to add parameters to pipelines, similar to what was done with tasks.

Go ahead and add a parameter to the same pipeline:

1. Add a `params` object to the `spec` section of your YAML file:

    ```
    spec:
      params:
    ```

2. Add a new parameter called `dice-sides` of the `string` type. You can give it the default value of `"6"`. The syntax for this parameter is the same as used for parameters added to tasks in the previous chapter:

    ```
    - name: dice-sides
      type: "string"
      default: "6"
      description: Number of sides on the dice
    ```

3. In the `roll` task, change the value of the `sides` parameter to use the value from the pipeline parameter:

    ```
    value: "$(params.dice-sides)"
    ```

4. This is what your final pipeline should look like:

    ```
    apiVersion: tekton.dev/v1beta1
    kind: Pipeline
    metadata:
      name: parametrized-dice-roll
    spec:
      params:
        - name: dice-sides
          type: "string"
          default: "6"
          description: Number of sides on the dice
      tasks:
        - name: first
          taskRef:
    ```

```
      name: first-task
  - name: roll
    params:
      - name: sides
        value: "$(params.dice-sides)"
    taskRef:
      name: die-roll-param
```

5. Apply this file and start the pipeline using the CLI. This time, `tkn` will ask you for the value to use for the `dice-sides` parameter:

```
$ kubectl apply -f ./parametrized-dice-roll-pipeline-
param.yaml
pipeline.tekton.dev/parametrized-dice-roll configured
```

```
$ tkn pipeline start parametrized-dice-roll --showlog
? Value for param `dice-sides` of type `string`? (Default
is `6`) 20
PipelineRun started: parametrized-dice-roll-run-gns9f
Waiting for logs to be available...
[first : unnamed-0] Hello from first task
[roll : greetings] Rolling 20-sided dice
[roll : generate-random-number] 12
```

6. You can also pass in the parameters directly from the CLI by using the `-p` argument with the key and value to be used by the PipelineRun. In the following example, `-p dice-sides=12` is passed to `tkn`, and the pipeline run is created with those values:

```
$ tkn pipeline start parametrized-dice-roll -p dice-
sides=12 --showlog
PipelineRun started: parametrized-dice-roll-run-jv5ml
Waiting for logs to be available...
[first : unnamed-0] Hello from first task
[roll : greetings] Rolling 12-sided dice
[roll : generate-random-number] 8
```

7. Finally, you can also create a pipeline run by using the default values directly using the `--use-param-default` flag, as shown here:

```
$ tkn pipeline start parametrized-dice-roll --use-param-
defaults --showlog
PipelineRun started: parametrized-dice-roll-run-s6ksl
Waiting for logs to be available...
[first : unnamed-0] Hello from first task
[roll : greetings] Rolling 6-sided dice
[roll : generate-random-number] 2
```

You now know how to use parameters to make your CI/CD pipelines more flexible and reusable across your various projects. Now that you know how to use parameters, you will see how you can reuse the same task across a single pipeline using different parameters.

Reusing tasks in the context of a pipeline

In the last chapter, you saw how to make tasks reusable by using parameters. You also saw how you can set the values for those parameters from a pipeline. Using those parameters, you can use a given task in multiple pipelines, and you can even use a given task inside a single pipeline. This is what you will do here:

1. Start with a new file called `log-task.yaml`. Here, create a new task called `logger`:

```
apiVersion: tekton.dev/v1beta1
kind: Task
metadata:
  name: logger
spec:
```

2. This task will need a parameter. You can give it the name `text`. This will be a parameter of the `string` type:

```
params:
  - name: text
    type: string
```

3. For the `steps` object, you will have a single step that logs the date and time
    followed by the text to be logged:

```
steps:
  - name: log
    image: registry.access.redhat.com/ubi8/ubi-minimal
    script: |
      DATE=$(date +%d/%m/%Y\ %T)
      echo [$DATE] - $(params.text)
```

You can now use this generic task every time you want to log something to the standard
output. You are now ready to create your new pipeline that will use this task multiple
times:

1. Start with a new pipeline called `task-reuse`, which can be stored in a file named
    `task-reuse.yaml`:

```
apiVersion: tekton.dev/v1beta1
kind: Pipeline
metadata:
  name: task-reuse
spec:
  tasks:
```

2. Next, add a first task. This task, called `say-hello`, uses the `logger` task with the
    parameter text set to `Hello`:

```
  - name: say-hello
    params:
      - name: text
        value: "Hello"
    taskRef:
      name: logger
```

3. Then, add a second task. This task uses the same `logger` task, but this time, the
    value field will be different:

```
  - name: log-something
    params:
      - name: text
        value: "Something else being logged"
```

```
        taskRef:
          name: logger
```

4. Apply the task and the pipeline to your Kubernetes cluster:

```
$ kubectl apply -f ./log-task.yaml
task.tekton.dev/logger created
$ kubectl apply -f ./task-reuse.yaml
pipeline.tekton.dev/task-reuse configured
```

5. You are now ready to start this new pipeline and look at the logs:

```
$ tkn pipeline start task-reuse --showlog
PipelineRun started: task-reuse-run-mhdcv
Waiting for logs to be available...
[say-hello : log] [09/03/2021 21:41:55] - Hello
[log-something : log] [09/03/2021 21:41:55] - Something
else being logged
```

> **Note**
>
> The order in which the logs are displayed might differ for you. More on that in the *Ordering tasks within pipelines* section.

You now know how to reuse a single task, not only across all of your CI/CD Tekton pipelines but also to perform different functions in a single pipeline. This can be useful when you have a tool that you want to reuse across your pipeline. For example, in a Node.js project, you could have a task that runs a configurable npm script. Then, in the pipeline, you would be able to use this npm task to install the packages, run unit tests, and build your application—all of that by using a single task.

Now that you know how to make the most of the tasks in a pipeline, let's see how the order in which each task runs can be changed.

Ordering tasks within pipelines

You might have noticed that the task-reuse tasks were coming out in a random order in the last section. Sometimes the say-hello task would run first, while other times it was the log-something task that was completed first. In that specific pipeline, it is tough to predict which task will complete in which order. When the pipeline run is created, the two pods are created at the same time.

In this case, the order in which Tekton executed the tasks didn't matter. Both tasks ran simultaneously in their own pod, and it ended up saving us some time in the total pipeline execution, as opposed to running them one after the other.

Sometimes, though, you will want the tasks to happen in a specific order. This will be especially true when a task produces an output required by a subsequent task.

To demonstrate this, we will create a new pipeline with a single task that we reuse multiple times. The task in question will have three steps. The first step is to log the start time, then there's a sleep step and a step to log the finish time.

Let's start with the new task:

1. In a file called `log-and-sleep.yaml`, create a new task with the name `log-and-sleep`:

    ```
    apiVersion: tekton.dev/v1beta1
    kind: Task
    metadata:
      name: sleep-and-log
    spec:
    ```

2. Next, add the parameters. This task will have two of them—a parameter with the task's name and another for the sleep timer's duration:

    ```
    params:
      - name: task-name
        type: string
      - name: time
        type: string
        default: "1"
    ```

3. Create the first step, which will echo the date and time, along with a message stating that the task was started:

    ```
    steps:
      - name: init
        image: registry.access.redhat.com/ubi8/ubi-minimal
        command:
          - /bin/bash
        args:
          - "-c"
    ```

```
    - "echo [$(date '+%d/%m/%Y %T')] - Task $(params.
task-name) Started"
```

4. Add another step that will sleep for the number of seconds specified in the associated parameter:

```
- name: sleep
  image: registry.access.redhat.com/ubi8/ubi-minimal
  command:
    - /bin/bash
  args:
    - -c
    - sleep $(params.time)
```

5. Add a final step to output a message with the date and time of the task completion:

```
- name: log
  image: registry.access.redhat.com/ubi8/ubi-minimal
  command:
    - /bin/bash
  args:
    - "-c"
    - "echo [$(date '+%d/%m/%Y %T')] - Task $(params.
task-name) Completed"
```

Now that the task is ready to be used by a pipeline, let's create a new pipeline that will use this single task multiple times:

1. In a file called ordered-tasks-pipeline.yaml, create a new pipeline called ordered-tasks-pipeline:

```
apiVersion: tekton.dev/v1beta1
kind: Pipeline
metadata:
  name: ordered-tasks
spec:
  tasks:
```

2. Add a task named `first`, which will reference the task named `sleep-and-log` with the A parameter value for `task-name` and 2 for `time`:

```
- name: first
  params:
    - name: task-name
      value: A
    - name: time
      value: "2"
  taskRef:
    name: sleep-and-log
```

3. Add a task named `second`, still using the same `sleep-and-log` task in reference. This one uses the default value for the time, and the value for `task-name` is B:

```
- name: second
  params:
    - name: task-name
      value: B
  taskRef:
    name: sleep-and-log
```

4. Add a third task using the same task reference again. This one will have `task-name` with the value C and a `time` value of 3:

```
- name: third
  params:
    - name: task-name
      value: C
    - name: time
      value: "3"
  taskRef:
    name: sleep-and-log
```

5. Add one last task called `fourth`. This one uses the default parameter value for `time`. The `task-name` parameter value is D:

```
- name: fourth
  params:
    - name: task-name
```

```
          value: D
      taskRef:
        name: sleep-and-log
```

6. Apply those files to your Kubernetes cluster:

```
$ kubectl apply -f ./sleep-and-log.yaml
task.tekton.dev/sleep-and-log created


$ kubectl apply -f ./ordered-tasks-pipeline.yaml
pipeline.tekton.dev/ordered-tasks created
```

7. Start the ordered-tasks pipeline using the tkn CLI tool:

```
$ tkn pipeline start ordered-tasks --showlog
PipelineRun started: ordered-tasks-run-vx4jt
Waiting for logs to be available...
[first : init] [12/03/2021 15:29:41] - Task A Started
[second : init] [12/03/2021 15:29:42] - Task B Started
[third : init] [12/03/2021 15:29:44] - Task C Started
[second : log] [12/03/2021 15:29:44] - Task B Completed
[first : log] [12/03/2021 15:29:44] - Task A Completed
[fourth : init] [12/03/2021 15:29:47] - Task D Started
[third : log] [12/03/2021 15:29:48] - Task C Completed
[fourth : log] [12/03/2021 15:29:48] - Task D Completed
```

Your resulting logs should be somewhat similar, but there is a good chance that they will differ. That is because Tekton tries to start all the tasks at the same time. As you can see in the results shown in the preceding code block, tasks A and B were completed before task D was started.

If you are using VS Code with the Tekton extension, you can use the Pipeline Preview feature to visualize your pipeline. To do so, use *Ctrl + Shift + P* and type in `Pipeline Preview`. Select the **Tekton: Open Pipeline Preview to the Side** option from the dropdown, and you should see the pipeline displayed as in the following screenshot:

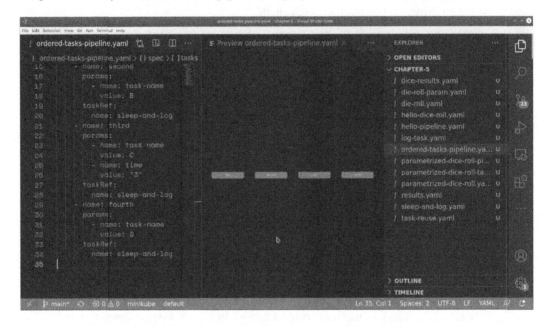

Figure 5.1 – Pipeline preview before ordering tasks

When you build your CI/CD pipelines, there is a good chance that you will want to run some tasks in parallel. For example, you could run a linting task and a unit testing task at the same time. This would cut down the execution time for your pipeline, and there is no need to wait for one to be completed before another.

You will have some cases where you want tasks to run in a specific order, though. By taking the same example, you will want to clone your source code from the Git repository and install all the dependencies before proceeding to your code's linting and testing.

The following screenshot represents such a pipeline:

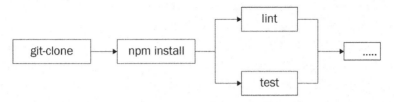

Figure 5.2 – A typical Node.js CI/CD pipeline

To specify the order of tasks, you can add the runAfter list to your task definitions in the pipeline.

Let's try to modify this pipeline so that each task runs in order:

1. In the second task, add a runAfter list with a single element with the value first:

    ```
    - name: second
      ...
      runAfter:
        - first
    ```

2. In the third task, add a runAfter list with the value second:

    ```
    - name: third
      ...
      runAfter:
        - second
    ```

3. In the last task, add a runAfter list as well so that this task runs after third:

    ```
    - name: fourth
      ...
      runAfter:
        - third
    ```

4. Apply this modified file to your cluster and start the pipeline using the tkn CLI tool:

    ```
    $ kubectl apply -f ./ordered-tasks-pipeline.yaml
    pipeline.tekton.dev/ordered-tasks configured
    ```

```
$ tkn pipeline start ordered-tasks --showlog
PipelineRun started: ordered-tasks-run-dptxs
Waiting for logs to be available...
[first : init] [12/03/2021 16:03:06] - Task A Started
[first : log] [12/03/2021 16:03:08] - Task A Completed
[second : init] [12/03/2021 16:03:17] - Task B Started
[second : log] [12/03/2021 16:03:18] - Task B Completed
[third : init] [12/03/2021 16:03:27] - Task C Started
[third : log] [12/03/2021 16:03:30] - Task C Completed
[fourth : init] [12/03/2021 16:03:38] - Task D Started
[fourth : log] [12/03/2021 16:03:39] - Task D Completed
```

This time, each task was started and completed before proceeding to the next one. This makes the outcome much more predictable than the original pipeline. On the other hand, you might have noticed that this pipeline took much longer to execute. If you look at the time difference between the first line logged and the last one, this one took 33 seconds, compared to 7 seconds in the first run, which ran all the tasks in parallel.

The pipeline preview from the Tekton extension in VS Code is shown in the following screenshot:

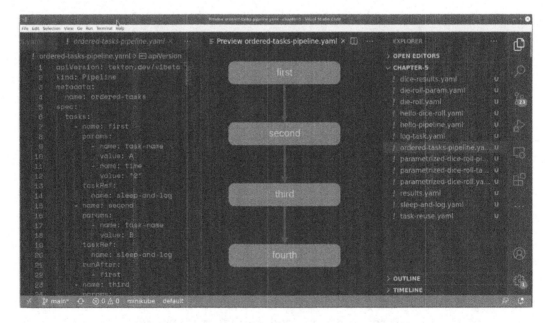

Figure 5.3 – Pipeline preview with tasks ordered sequentially

Your pipelines don't need to run everything in parallel or everything in sequence. You can use a mix of both. Because the `runAfter` field is a list, you can wait for more than one task to be completed before proceeding to the next one.

Let's edit this pipeline one last time. For this next run, tasks B and C will run after A is completed, and task D will run after B and C are done:

1. Change the `third` task to run after the `first` one:

```
- name: third
  ...
  runAfter:
    - first
```

2. Change the `fourth` task to run after both the `second` and `third` tasks have been completed:

```
- name: fourth
  ...
  runAfter:
    - second
    - third
```

3. Apply the `ordered-tasks-pipeline.yaml` file to your cluster and start the pipeline one more time:

```
$ kubectl apply -f ./ordered-tasks-pipeline.yaml
pipeline.tekton.dev/ordered-tasks configured

$ tkn pipeline start ordered-tasks --showlog
PipelineRun started: ordered-tasks-run-mpxcl
Waiting for logs to be available...
[first : init] [12/03/2021 16:38:26] - Task A Started
[first : log] [12/03/2021 16:38:29] - Task A Completed
[second : init] [12/03/2021 16:38:40] - Task B Started
[third : init] [12/03/2021 16:38:41] - Task C Started
[second : log] [12/03/2021 16:38:41] - Task B Completed
[third : log] [12/03/2021 16:38:44] - Task C Completed
[fourth : init] [12/03/2021 16:38:52] - Task D Started
[fourth : log] [12/03/2021 16:38:53] - Task D Completed
```

This time, task A was completed before B and C were started. Only after those two tasks were completed will task D start. The total duration for this run was 27 seconds. A few seconds were shaved off the total execution time thanks to running two of the tasks in parallel.

If you look at the pipeline preview in VS Code, you will be able to visualize this:

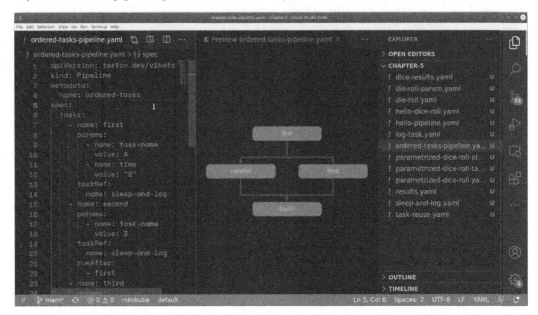

Figure 5.4 – The Pipeline Preview screen with a mix of parallel and sequential tasks

Now that you know how to arrange tasks in a pipeline, you will be able to start sharing information across the various tasks. This will be introduced in the next section.

Using task results in pipelines

In the previous chapter, you've seen how to use results inside tasks to share information across steps. You can also use the same results to share limited information across tasks.

For the last example in this chapter, you will rewrite the `dice-roll` task to produce a result instead of echoing the result. This randomly generated number will then be picked up by the `logger` task to be displayed:

1. Start by creating a file named `dice-results.yaml` in which you will create the base of your new task named `dice-roll-result`:

    ```
    apiVersion: tekton.dev/v1beta1
    kind: Task
    ```

```
metadata:
   name: dice-roll-result
spec:
```

2. Just like you did in the previous version of the die-roll task, add a parameter with a default value of "6":

```
params:
   - name: sides
     description: Number of sides to the dice
     default: "6"
     type: string
```

3. Define a result called dice-roll and give it a description:

```
results:
   - name: dice-roll
     description: Random number generated by the dice
 roll
```

4. Add a single step that will use a Node.js image and run a script to generate a random number:

```
steps:
   - name: generate-random-number
     image: node:14
     script: |
       #!/usr/bin/env node
       const fs = require("fs");
       const max = $(params.sides)
       let randomNumber = Math.floor(Math.random() *
 max) + 1;
```

5. Finish that script with the following line of code that will write the randomNumber value into a file located at $(results.dice-roll.path). Tekton will do a variable substitution there to inject the actual path of the result file. Once the write operation is completed, a callback function is run and outputs a confirmation message:

```
       fs.writeFile("$(results.dice-roll.path)",
 randomNumber.toString(), () => {
```

```
        console.log("Dice rolled");
    });
```

This task is now ready to be used in your pipeline. As opposed to an earlier version of this script, the dice roll results are never displayed by this task. Instead, we will use the same `logger` task that was created earlier to output the result. This will all be done in the following new pipeline:

1. In a file called `results.yaml`, create a new pipeline named `results`:

    ```
    apiVersion: tekton.dev/v1beta1
    kind: Pipeline
    metadata:
      name: results
    spec:
    ```

2. This pipeline will have a single parameter for the number of sides of the die. This will later be passed to the task:

    ```
    params:
      - name: sides
        default: "6"
        type: "string"
    ```

3. Add a first task that will log some text to indicate that the die is about to be rolled. The `text` parameter value will do a variable substitution to indicate the number of sides specified when the pipeline run was created:

    ```
    tasks:
      - name: intro
        params:
          - name: text
            value: "Preparing to roll the $(params.sides)-
    sided dice"
        taskRef:
          name: logger
    ```

> **Note**
>
> This task references the task created in the *Reusing tasks in the context of a pipeline* section of this chapter.

4. Add another task that will reference the newly created `dice-roll-result` task. It will take the `sides` parameter from the pipeline and inject it as the task parameter of the same name. This task should run after the `intro` task:

```
- name: roll
  params:
    - name: sides
      value: $(params.sides)
  taskRef:
    name: dice-roll-result
  runAfter:
    - intro
```

5. Add a final task that references the `logger` task again. This time, you will indicate the result from the previous step. You can use a variable substitution here by using `task.<task name>.results.<result name>`. This task needs a `runAfter` list as well. Without it, the result won't be available, and the pipeline will break:

```
- name: result
  params:
    - name: text
      value: "Result from dice roll was $(tasks.roll.
results.dice-roll)"
  taskRef:
    name: logger
  runAfter:
    - roll
```

6. Apply these two new files to your cluster:

```
$ kubectl apply -f ./dice-results.yaml
task.tekton.dev/dice-roll-result created


$ kubectl apply -f ./results.yaml
pipeline.tekton.dev/results created
```

7. Start the pipeline using the `tkn` CLI tool:

```
$ tkn pipeline start results --showlog
? Value for param `sides` of type `string`? (Default is
`6`) 20
PipelineRun started: results-run-lvfm4
Waiting for logs to be available...
[intro : log] [12/03/2021 20:15:32] - Preparing to roll
the 20-sided dice
[roll : generate-random-number] Dice rolled
[result : log] [12/03/2021 20:15:44] - Result from dice
roll was 12
```

In this last example, the number was generated by the `roll` task, then stored in a file that was later retrieved by the last task, called `result`. By using results, you can now share information across various tasks. Keep in mind that results are limited to 4 KB, though.

Now that you know how Tekton pipelines use tasks to create CI/CD pipelines, let's look at the pipeline executions called pipeline runs.

Introducing pipeline runs

Pipeline runs are to pipelines what task runs are to tasks. They are the actual executions of the pipelines.

Using the pipeline used in the last section, let's create a new pipeline run and examine the output:

```
$ tkn pipeline start results
? Value for param `sides` of type `string`? (Default is `6`) 6
PipelineRun started: results-run-sb6lk


In order to track the PipelineRun progress run:
tkn pipelinerun logs results-run-sb6lk -f -n default
```

You can see that when you run the `tkn pipeline start` command, it generates a pipeline run with a random name. In this case, the name is `results-run-sb6lk`. To see the output of the run, you will use the `tkn` CLI tool to visualize the logs of this specific pipeline run.

Because pipeline runs are Kubernetes objects, you can manipulate them with `kubectl` the same way you would any other Kubernetes primitive. For example, you could use `kubectl get` to list all the pipeline runs that exist inside your cluster:

```
$ kubectl get pipelineruns
NAME                      SUCCEEDED   REASON
STARTTIME    COMPLETIONTIME
app-deploy-run-5d27c      False       Failed
3d15h        3d15h
level-selector-run-ljlqh  True        Succeeded
42h          42h
ordered-tasks-run-vx4jt   True        Succeeded
45h          45h
results-run-sb6lk         True        Succeeded
2m17s        117s
```

If you find that you have too many of them, you can also delete some using the `kubectl` CLI tool. Using `labels` in the `metadata` section of your object definitions would help filter out those you want to include in your queries:

```
$ kubectl delete pipelinerun results-run-s8w2j
pipelinerun.tekton.dev "results-run-s8w2j" deleted
```

Similar to what you did with task runs, you can also see the full YAML definition of the `pipelinerun`:

```
$ kubectl get pipelinerun results-run-sb6lk -o yaml
```

You will find a lot of information about the pipeline run here. First, start by looking at the `spec` field:

```
spec:
  params:
  - name: sides
    value: "6"
  pipelineRef:
    name: results
  serviceAccountName: default
  timeout: 1h0m0s
```

You can see here which pipeline was used as a reference for this pipeline run and the values of the parameters you used for this run. This can be useful to track the inputs of your pipeline if the outcome is not as expected.

After the `spec` field, you will see the status of the pipeline execution. There, you will find information about the actual execution, such as the start and completion times. You will also find the entire pipeline `spec` definition. If you scroll down, you will also find a `taskRuns` list:

```
taskRuns:
  results-run-k4qc7-intro-z4vg5:
    pipelineTaskName: intro
    status:
      completionTime: "2021-03-14T12:43:07Z"
      conditions:
      - lastTransitionTime: "2021-03-14T12:43:07Z"
        message: All Steps have completed executing
        reason: Succeeded
        status: "True"
        type: Succeeded
      podName: results-run-k4qc7-intro-z4vg5-pod-g9wc5
```

For each task inside the pipeline, a `taskrun` was also created. You can see the status of each step of each task directly in the `pipelinerun` YAML object. If something would've halted the pipeline's execution, you would be able to find it here.

In addition to all this information, you can also find the outputs of the `taskruns` in this object. For example, the `roll` task of the `results` pipeline generated a `result`. If you look at the `taskRuns` section of the object, you can see the actual task results passed to the next tasks:

```
  results-run-k4qc7-roll-nss45:
    pipelineTaskName: roll
    ...
      taskResults:
      - name: dice-roll
        value: "5"
```

The YAML output of your pipeline run contains a lot of valuable information to try and debug a failing pipeline, but it can be somewhat difficult to read through it. Thankfully, you can use visualization tools to make it easier to decipher that information. **Tekton Dashboard** provides you with the same information in a more visual way, as seen in the following screenshot:

Figure 5.5 – PipelineRun viewed in Tekton Dashboard

Should you prefer to stay in the comfort of your IDE, you can also use the Tekton extension in VS Code to see the pipeline execution results by opening up the side panel and selecting the matching pipeline run, as seen in the following screenshot:

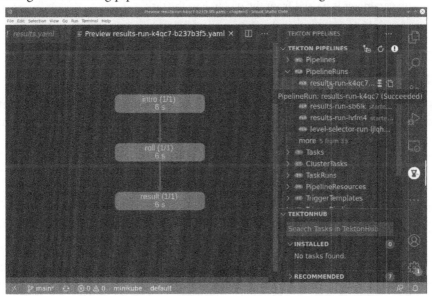

Figure 5.6 – Visualizing the PipelineRun in VS Code

Take some time to go through the content of the YAML files. Being able to analyze those files is key to being able to debug failing Tekton pipelines.

Now that you know everything needed about pipelines, it is time to start building your own.

Getting your hands dirty

Once again, it is time for you to test out those newly learned skills. You can find a solution to these problems in the *Assessments* chapter of this book. These challenges will use the concepts that you have seen in this chapter.

Back to the basics

For your first challenge, start by building a pipeline that will output a `hello` message. To do so, use the task called `logger` that you created in this chapter. The pipeline will take a parameter to indicate who to say hello to, which should default to `World`. Run this pipeline with different parameter values using the CLI. Run it with the default values. Do one last run with the parameter value specified in the CLI command directly.

> Tips
> - This pipeline has a single task.
> - The parameter is passed from the pipeline to the task.
> - Reuse the previously created task logger.

Counting files in a repo

For this next challenge, build a pipeline that will clone a Git repository and then output the number of files found in that repository. Use the `logger` task to output the number of files.

> Tips
> - You will need to use a result to pass information to the logger task.
> - The result is limited to 4 KB; therefore, your task will need to clone and then count the files.
> - The `alpine/git` image is a minimal image that includes the Git CLI tool.
> - You can use the `ls | wc -l` command to count the number of files.
> - The order in which the tasks will run is important here.

Weather services

For this last challenge, build a pipeline that gets weather information and outputs only the current temperature. You can use the website wttr.in to get the weather data in a text format that you can then process. The name of the city should be a parameter. You will use the weather service result in a second task to extract only the current temperature. Finally, use the `logger` task to output the temperature.

> **Tips**
>
> - You will have three tasks that need to run to display the final temperature.
>
> - Using `curl wttr.in/<City>?format=4` will provide you with limited weather information for any `<City>` argument.
>
> - To extract the third column in the weather results (the column that contains the current temperature), you can use awk `'{print $3}'`.

Summary

You now know everything there is to know about pipelines and how you can use them to run various tasks. You've seen how you can pass parameters across the tasks. You have also seen how tasks can be reused with different parameters to produce different outputs.

You can run those tasks either in parallel or in sequence, and you've seen how to use a mix of both to make your pipelines more efficient.

After you learned how to order your tasks, you saw how tasks can output some results that can then be used by a task that comes later in the pipeline execution.

You have also learned how to analyze pipeline runs and visualize them to help you find what is wrong with your pipeline executions when they fail. In the next chapter, you will learn more advanced techniques to debug your tasks and pipelines.

6
Debugging and Cleaning Up Pipelines and Tasks

In the previous chapters, all of your pipelines ran successfully. However, when you start implementing your Tekton **continuous integration/continuous deployment (CI/CD)** pipelines, chances are that this won't run as smoothly. There is a fair possibility that some of the tasks will fail at times, and that is a good thing. If you have a task running unit tests on your code base, you will want it to fail and stop the pipeline so that a broken version of your application is not deployed in production.

In this chapter, you will see what happens when a task in a pipeline fails. You will also learn a few techniques to investigate those failures. And finally, you will learn about... finally, a new concept that can be used as part of your pipelines to clean up your environment to get ready for the next run.

In this chapter, we are going to cover the following main topics:

- Debugging pipelines
- Running a halting task

- Adding a `finally` task
- Getting your hands dirty

Technical requirements

You can find all of the examples described in this chapter in the `chapter-6` folder of the GitHub repository, found at `https://github.com/PacktPublishing/Building-CI-CD-systems-using-Tekton`.

You can also see the *Code in Action* videos at the following link: `https://bit.ly/3eWxaOo`

Debugging pipelines

As you build your first pipelines, you will inevitably encounter some issues. Writing pipeline definitions without getting a failing pod is just as likely as writing a piece of software without running into a bug, yet there are ways to figure out what is happening inside those pods and potentially identify issues that are causing the pipeline to break.

Let's start by creating a first task that will intentionally fail. This task will have a non-existing base image for one of the steps, and you will see how you can debug this issue when the pipeline stalls:

1. In a file named `invalid-image-task.yaml`, add a new task called `invalid-image`:

```
apiVersion: tekton.dev/v1beta1
kind: Task
metadata:
  name: invalid-image
spec:
  steps:
```

2. Add a single step called `log`, which will use an invalid image name:

```
    - name: log
      image: invaliduser/nonexistingimage
```

3. To be compliant with the task definition, add a command to echo some message:

```
command:
  - /bin/bash
args: ['-c', 'echo "this task will fail"']
```

4. Now that you have a task you know will fail, create a new pipeline. In a file named `failing-pipeline.yaml`, add a pipeline named `failing`:

```
apiVersion: tekton.dev/v1beta1
kind: Pipeline
metadata:
  name: failing
```

5. In the `spec` field, add a `tasks` list:

```
spec:
  tasks:
```

6. This pipeline will have a single task called `fail` that references the `invalid-image` task:

```
  - name: fail
    taskRef:
      name: invalid-image
```

7. Apply those two files and start the pipeline:

```
$ kubectl apply -f ./invalid-image-task.yaml
task.tekton.dev/invalid-image created

$ kubectl apply -f ./failing-pipeline.yaml
pipeline.tekton.dev/failing created

$ tkn pipeline start failing --showlog
PipelineRun started: failing-run-jldmw
Waiting for logs to be available...
```

If you used the `--showlog` flag as I did here, it would seem as though your pipeline froze, which is exactly the case. Use *Ctrl + C* to stop waiting for those logs, and let's see how to figure out what is happening inside the pipeline.

The first thing to do would be to look for the pipeline run. You can do this with the `tkn` **command-line interface (CLI)** tool:

```
$ tkn pipelinerun ls
NAME STARTED DURATION STATUS
failing-run-jldmw 2 minutes ago --- Running
```

From the output of the previous command, you can see that you have a pipeline run that is currently running. Maybe it is just taking longer than expected. You can examine the logs for that pipeline again by using the `tkn` CLI tool along with the name of the `pipelinerun` object:

```
$ tkn pipelinerun logs failing-run-jldmw
Pipeline still running ...
```

Still nothing. The pipeline hasn't produced any output so far, and it's been a few minutes already. There is probably something going on, then. You can use *Ctrl + C* to stop waiting for those logs. This time, you will look at the pods.

When a PipelineRun is created, it will generate a pod for each of the tasks in the pipeline definition. This means that you can use `kubectl` to see the status of the pods. The pod will be named `<pipelineName>-run-<randomId>-<taskName>-<randomId>-pod-<randomId>`. In this case, the pipeline run that is failing has the ID `jldmw`, which means that you should be looking for pods called `failing-run-jldmw-fail-xxxxx-pod-xxxxx`. This will help you find the pod that is crashing your pipeline.

Using `kubectl`, find the matching pod:

```
$ kubectl get pods
NAME READY STATUS RESTARTS AGE
failing-run-jldmw-fail-58ng8-pod-9rtx5 0/1 ImagePullBackOff 0
9m5s
```

You can already see that there is a problem with pulling the image for this pod. To get more details, you can use `kubectl describe`:

```
$ kubectl describe pod/failing-run-jldmw-fail-58ng8-pod-9rtx5
Name: failing-run-jldmw-fail-58ng8-pod-9rtx5
...
Status: Pending
...
Events:
```

```
Type Reason Age From Message
---- ------ ---- ---- -------
...
Normal Pulling 8m40s (x4 over 10m) kubelet Pulling image
"invaliduser/nonexistingimage"
  Warning Failed 8m39s (x4 over 10m) kubelet Failed to pull
image "invaliduser/nonexistingimage": rpc error: code = Unknown
desc = Error response from daemon: pull access denied for
invaliduser/nonexistingimage, repository does not exist or
may require 'docker login': denied: requested access to the
resource is denied
  Warning Failed 8m39s (x4 over 10m) kubelet Error:
ErrImagePull
  Warning Failed 8m26s (x5 over 10m) kubelet Error:
ImagePullBackOff
  Normal BackOff 4m59s (x20 over 10m) kubelet Back-off pulling
image "invaliduser/nonexistingimage"
```

This command will return a lot of information. The important part in this output is the Events section. In here, you can see that the pod tried to pull the image but failed. More specifically, you can see the following error message:

```
Error response from daemon: pull access denied for invaliduser/
nonexistingimage, repository does not exist or may require
'docker login'
```

This gives you some hints on what happened here. Perhaps there is a typo in the image name, or maybe you are trying to access a private image without logging in to your registry. Either way, you have found the reason why this pipeline run was stalled.

You can force the pipeline run to stop by using the cancel command:

```
$ tkn pipelinerun cancel failing-run-jldmw
PipelineRun cancelled: failing-run-jldmw
```

If you run a ls command to see the status of your pipeline run you should see that tkn stopped it:

```
$ tkn pipelinerun ls
NAME STARTED DURATION STATUS
failing-run-jldmw 16 minutes ago 16 minutes
Cancelled(PipelineRunCancelled)
```

Task runs will run for 1 hour before they time out by default, which is why you were able to look at the pods and see what was happening. Once they time out, the pod is then terminated and deleted, and you won't be able to see the events in the pod description. If you want to change the time limit to a shorter duration, you can change this by adding a timeout field to the pipeline's tasks definition:

```
apiVersion: tekton.dev/v1beta1
kind: Pipeline
metadata:
  name: failing
spec:
  tasks:
    - name: fail
      timeout: "0h0m30s"
      taskRef:
        name: invalid-image
```

Try applying this file to your cluster and running the pipeline once more:

```
$ kubectl apply -f ./failing-pipeline.yaml
pipeline.tekton.dev/failing configured

$ tkn pipeline start failing --showlog
PipelineRun started: failing-run-hbpl7
Waiting for logs to be available...
failed to get logs for task fail : task fail failed: failed to
run the pod failing-run-hbpl7-fail-4jk57-pod-681j8. Run tkn tr
desc failing-run-hbpl7-fail-4jk57 for more details.
failed to get logs for task fail : error in getting logs
for step log: error getting logs for pod failing-run-hbpl7-
fail-4jk57-pod-681j8(step-log) : container "step-log" in pod
"failing-run-hbpl7-fail-4jk57-pod-681j8" is waiting to start:
trying and failing to pull image
```

After 30 seconds an error message should be displayed, giving you hints about why the task failed. This is another way to find out useful information about why your pods are not working as expected.

Using a combination of `tkn pipelinerun describe`, `kubectl describe pods`, and `timeouts`, you should now be able to find out why your pipelines are not configured correctly. Sometimes, you will also need to understand why they are stopping during execution, and that is what you will see in the next section.

Running a halting task

Your pipelines are there to help you automate the delivery mechanisms of your applications. The ultimate goal is to make it possible to ship faster and more frequently. On the other hand, you also want to avoid pushing code that is broken or that doesn't pass your standards. This is why you will sometimes have some pipeline runs that won't complete. If you have a task running some failing unit tests, Tekton should not start the deployment task.

To demonstrate this, you will create a task that logs some text and then uses a specific exit code to tell Tekton whether the task succeeded or not.

> **Note**
>
> Normally, the executable running inside a step would provide the exit code. For those codes, 0 indicates success, while any other number indicates some failure.

You will then build a pipeline using that task to simulate failing tasks inside a CI/CD pipeline:

1. Create a new file named `log-and-exit.yaml` in which you create a new task called `log-and-exit`:

```yaml
apiVersion: tekton.dev/v1beta1
kind: Task
metadata:
  name: log-and-exit
spec:
```

2. For this task, you will need two parameters—one for the text to echo and another parameter for the exit code to be used:

```yaml
params:
  - name: text
    type: string
```

```
   - name: exitcode
     type: string
```

3. The first step of this task uses a **Universal Base Image (UBI)** to echo the content of the text parameter:

```
steps:
  - name: log
    image: registry.access.redhat.com/ubi8/ubi
    command:
      - /bin/bash
    args: ["-c", " echo $(params.text)"]
```

4. The second step will run the exit command with the error code provided in the parameters:

```
  - name: exit
    image: registry.access.redhat.com/ubi8/ubi
    command:
      - /bin/bash
    args: ["-c", "echo 'Exiting with code $(params.exitcode)' && exit $(params.exitcode)"]
```

5. Next, in a file named exitcodes.yaml, create a new pipeline called exitcodes:

```
apiVersion: tekton.dev/v1beta1
kind: Pipeline
metadata:
  name: exitcodes
spec:
  tasks:
```

6. The first task will use the log-and-exit task and will simulate a git clone operation. The task will have a text parameter with the value Simulating git clone and an exitcode parameter with the value 0:

```
  - name: clone
    taskRef:
      name: log-and-exit
    params:
      - name: text
```

```
        value: "Simulating git clone"
    - name: exitcode
        value: "0"
```

7. The next task will use the same task reference. This one will output a message
    indicating that this is a simulated unit test operation. It will also produce an exit
    code of 0. This task would need to run after the `clone` task:

```
- name: unit-tests
  taskRef:
    name: log-and-exit
  params:
    - name: text
        value: "Simulating unit testing"
    - name: exitcode
        value: "0"
  runAfter:
    - clone
```

8. Create a last task to output a message indicating a simulated deployment. The exit
    code should also be 0 for now. This task should run after `unit-tests`:

```
- name: deploy
  taskRef:
    name: log-and-exit
  params:
    - name: text
        value: "Simulating deployment"
    - name: exitcode
        value: "0"
  runAfter:
    - unit-tests
```

9. Apply those two files and start this pipeline:

```
$ kubectl apply -f ./log-and-exit.yaml
task.tekton.dev/log-and-exit created

$ kubectl apply -f ./exitcodes.yaml
```

```
pipeline.tekton.dev/exitcodes created


$ tkn pipeline start exitcodes --showlog
tkn pipeline start exitcodes --showlog
PipelineRun started: exitcodes-run-pg94f
Waiting for logs to be available...
[clone : log] Simulating git clone
[clone : exit] Exiting with code 0
[unit-tests : log] Simulating unit testing
[unit-tests : exit] Exiting with code 0
[deploy : log] Simulating deployment
[deploy : exit] Exiting with code 0
```

So far, everything looks good. The simulation pipeline has successfully deployed the application. Now, go back to the exitcodes.yaml file and change the exit code for the unit-tests task:

```
- name: unit-tests
  taskRef:
    name: log-and-exit
  params:
    - name: text
      value: "Simulating unit testing"
    - name: exitcode
      value: "1"
  runAfter:
    - clone
```

This will simulate another pipeline run where the unit-tests task will find an issue and return an error code. Apply this new file and rerun the pipeline:

```
$ kubectl apply -f ./exitcodes.yaml
pipeline.tekton.dev/exitcodes configured


$ tkn pipeline start exitcodes --showlog
PipelineRun started: exitcodes-run-pdv5x
Waiting for logs to be available...
[clone : log] Simulating git clone
```

```
[clone : exit] Exiting with code 0

[unit-tests : log] Simulating unit testing

[unit-tests : exit] Exiting with code 1

failed to get logs for task unit-tests : container step-
exit has failed : [{"key":"StartedAt","value":"2021-03-
19T17:41:13.052Z","type":"InternalTektonResult"}]
```

This time, it seems that there was an error. The unit tests failed. As you can see, the pipeline halted immediately; therefore, Tekton did not deploy the application in production. This CI/CD pipeline just enabled you to avoid deploying a broken application into production.

The only problem now is that you still need to find out what happened to the application. The tkn CLI tool can provide you with valuable information to track down the cause of this failure. Try using the tool to describe the pipelinerun object:

```
$ tkn pipelinerun describe exitcodes-run-pdv5x

Name: exitcodes-run-pdv5x

...

 Status

STARTED DURATION STATUS

2 minutes ago 11 seconds Failed

 Message

Tasks Completed: 2 (Failed: 1, Cancelled 0), Skipped: 1
("step-exit" exited with code 1 (image: "docker-pullable:
//registry.access.redhat.com/ubi8/ubi@sha256:aec01a874399c3a3
c31033b35761b28aef605504ade888f98f637442cc56b5c0"); for logs
run: kubectl -n default logs exitcodes-run-pdv5x-unit-tests
-h722m-pod-n5n77 -c step-exit
)

...

 Taskruns

NAME TASK NAME STARTED DURATION STATUS

· exitcodes-run-pdv5x-unit-tests-h722m unit-tests 2 minutes ago
6 seconds Failed

· exitcodes-run-pdv5x-clone-5mn8j clone 2 minutes ago 5 seconds
Succeeded
```

Using the `describe` command, you can find everything related to your `pipelineruns`. Some of the code was removed here for readability purposes, but you should be able to see the parameters that were passed in or the workspaces that were in use.

In this case, what you are interested in is the `Message` section. You can see here that a task failed (`unit-tests`) and that another one was skipped (`deploy`). You can also find a `kubectl` command that you could potentially run to see what happened. If you run this command you will see all the logs produced by this specific step:

```
$ kubectl -n default logs exitcodes-run-pdv5x-unit-tests-h722m-
pod-n5n77 -c step-exit
Exiting with code 1
```

Our simulated task did not produce a lot of output, but if this had been a real unit test run you should have been able to see the logs, along with the status of each unit test. This should help you find out which of the tests failed, and you could then fix it.

Once again, using a combination of `tkn` and `kubectl`, you can find out what is going on with your tasks and how you can fix them. You've also seen how the pipeline run stopped once it encountered a failing task. All subsequent tasks were skipped. This is great to avoid deploying a broken application, but sometimes you still need to perform an operation at the end of your pipeline. This would call for a `finally` object.

Adding a finally task

So far, all the pipelines that you built did not persist any data. Once the pods were terminated everything was taken down with them, and the next run always started from a fresh environment.

This won't always be the case. Most of the time, you will clone a code repository and store it on a **PersistentVolumeClaim** (**PVC**) for all tasks to access it. This exact scenario will be introduced in *Chapter 7, Sharing Data with Workspaces*. When you start using workspaces, you will need to clean up your persisted data to start with a clean environment each time. This is where `finally` tasks will come into play.

Those tasks will always be executed, even after there was a task that failed in the pipeline. Let's demonstrate this:

1. Create a new file called `cleanup.yaml` and create a task called `cleanup`:

    ```yaml
    apiVersion: tekton.dev/v1beta1
    kind: Task
    ```

```
metadata:
  name: cleanup
spec:
```

2. This task has a single step named `clean`. It uses a UBI to execute an `echo` command:

```
steps:
  - name: clean
    image: registry.access.redhat.com/ubi8/ubi
    command:
      - /bin/bash
    args: ['-c', 'echo Cleaning up!']
```

3. Copy the content from `exitcodes.yaml` into a new file called `exitcodes-finally.yaml`. At the end of the file, add a new object called `finally`:

```
apiVersion: tekton.dev/v1beta1
kind: Pipeline
metadata:
  name: exitcodes
spec:
  tasks:

    ...
  finally:
    - name: cleanup-task
      taskRef:
        name: cleanup
```

4. Apply those two files and start the `exitcodes` pipeline again by running the following commands in your terminal:

```
$ kubectl apply -f ./cleanup.yaml
task.tekton.dev/cleanup created


$ kubectl apply -f ./exitcodes-finally.yaml
pipeline.tekton.dev/exitcodes configured


$ tkn pipeline start exitcodes --showlog
PipelineRun started: exitcodes-run-nkv55
```

```
Waiting for logs to be available...
[clone : log] Simulating git clone
[clone : exit] Exiting with code 0
[unit-tests : log] Simulating unit testing
[unit-tests : exit] Exiting with code 1
[cleanup-task : clean] Cleaning up!
```

Once the unit-tests task failed again, you can see that the pipeline still ran the cleanup task instead of simply stopping. If you change the exit code in the unit-tests task to 0 and start the run again, you will see that the pipeline will perform the cleanup task once again.

The finally task will be performed on every execution of the pipeline.

Getting your hands dirty

Now that you know everything there is to know about debugging pipelines and the finally object, you are ready to tackle these exercises. These two exercises focus on knowledge you have gained in this chapter.

You will find a solution to these exercises in the *Assessments* section at the end of the book.

Fail if root

Create a pipeline with a simple task. This task will check if it is running as the root user. If the container is indeed running as the root user, the task will fail.

Tips
- The UBI runs as root.
- You will need some Bash scripting in your task to validate if $(whoami) is root.
- Use the exit command to indicate that the task succeeded or failed.

Make your bets

Imagine a game of Blackjack. The current hand value is 17. Draw a random card with a value between 1 and 10 and add it to the current hand. The value should be passed to the second task as a result. If the value is 21 or less, you win, and the task should complete successfully. If the value is higher than 21, it should fail. After the game, clean up the table.

> **Tips**
>
> - You need three tasks. The first one generates a random number, the second one adds it to 17 and returns an appropriate exit code, and the third one could use a `logger` task to output a message.
>
> - Use a `finally` task for the last one.
>
> - You can use a mix of Bash scripting or Node.js scripting to generate a card and add them.

Summary

When you start writing your first tasks and pipelines, you can expect them to fail at times. This might be expected, but sometimes it won't be. In this chapter, you've learned all the necessary tools to find out what is going on and how you can fix those issues.

You have also seen that a task failure can be a good thing, preventing you from accidentally deploying a broken version of your application. You have also learned how to find what caused those failures.

Finally, you've seen how to run a final task to clean up your work once the pipeline execution is completed. While this hasn't been very useful so far, you will need to use this concept when you start using workspaces. These will be introduced in the next chapter.

7
Sharing Data with Workspaces

In the last few chapters, you've seen some of Tekton's basic elements. With Tekton installed on your Kubernetes cluster, you can create tasks, which are small operations that you can perform as part of a pipeline. You've also seen how you can chain those tasks as part of a more extensive pipeline. So far, the examples that you've built have been relatively simple. The main limitation, for now, had to do with sharing data across the tasks. You've seen how to use results to transmit small bits of data, but you will need to share entire code bases if you want to automate operations on them. This is a job for workspaces, and you will learn how to use them in this chapter.

First, you will see how to use workspaces in the context of a single task. Using a workspace like this will let you share a volume across all the steps that compose your task. In this volume, you will be able to put larger pieces of data than you were able to with results. In order to bind workspaces with your tasks, you will also learn how to create a task run directly with a YAML file.

Once you are comfortable with these concepts, you will see how to use a workspace to share data across all the tasks inside a single pipeline. So far, you have only been able to share small bits of data, but using a workspace will enable you to share multiple files such as a full code base. This data can be persisted forever or cleaned up once a pipeline is completed. To do so, you will use a `finally` task, as you learned to do in the previous chapter.

Finally, you will learn more advanced techniques with workspaces, such as binding the workspaces directly in a pipeline run YAML file and using volume claim templates to dynamically create a persistent volume claim for your pipeline runs.

In this chapter, we are going to cover the following main topics:

- Introducing workspaces
- Types of volume sources
- Using your first workspace
- Using workspaces with task runs
- Adding a workspace to a pipeline
- Persisting data within a pipeline
- Cleaning up with finally
- Using workspaces in pipeline runs
- Using volume claim templates
- Getting your hands dirty

Technical requirements

You can find all of the examples described in this chapter in the `chapter-7` folder of the Git repository: `https://github.com/PacktPublishing/Building-CI-CD-systems-using-Tekton`.

You can also see the code in action videos at: `https://bit.ly/3kRAKNA`

Introducing workspaces

Workspaces are shared volumes used to transfer data between the various steps of a task. When authoring a new task to be used by your team, this has the benefit of making your tasks more flexible and reusable in different contexts. Using workspaces, your tasks' users will pick the type of volume they want to use for this volume.

You can also use workspaces to share data across tasks in a Tekton pipeline. This will come in handy when you want to share multiple files across the various steps of a pipeline. So far, you've used results to exchange small bits of information limited to 4,096 bytes, but eventually, you will want to share code bases and images, and this will be done with a workspace.

Types of volume sources

Workspaces need some sort of volume to mount the files to be shared. These types of volumes are called `VolumeSources`. The volume source you will use with your workspace will depend on the goals you want to achieve. The examples that will follow in this chapter will mainly target `emptyDir` and persistent volume claims. Still, four different sources are available to you when you author your tasks and pipelines.

emptyDir

`emptyDir` is, as the name suggests, an **empty directory** that is attached to a task run. This temporary folder should only be used in the context of a task and is not suitable to share information across tasks in a pipeline. It is, however, a straightforward mechanism that you can use to share data across steps in a task. This approach should be prioritized over using the home folder, as demonstrated in *Chapter 4, Stepping into Tasks*.

ConfigMap

The config map source lets your users use a Kubernetes-native **ConfigMap** object as a workspace. You've seen in *Chapter 4, Stepping into Tasks*, how you can mount a configuration map as a volume. Setting up a ConfigMap workspace will work in a very similar fashion. The configurations will be available as files in the mounted volume and available in read-only mode exclusively.

Secret

A workspace can also have a volume source type set to secret. This volume source enables you to use a Kubernetes `Secret` object. This object will be mounted just like a config map would and is also only available as a read-only volume.

Persistent volume claims and volume claim templates

To share a folder across your tasks that can be mounted as a writable file system, you will need to use a persistent volume claim. When you start a pipeline or a task that requires a persistent volume claim, you have the option to use an existing Persistent Volume Claim (PVC) that is available in your cluster. When using a persistent volume claim, only one run at a time will be able to use the volume. You could also use a `volumeClaimTemplate` in your task run or pipeline run. In this case, a PVC would be created and automatically be deleted once the run is deleted. It would also have the added benefit that you can run multiple pipelines at once.

When using persisted data, it will be your responsibility to manage the lifecycle of this data. If you use an existing PVC, you might need to use a `finally` task to clean everything up once you are done. Similarly, you will also need to ensure that the order in which your tasks access the file system is correct.

Now that you are more familiar with workspaces and their different flavors, you are ready to explore how to use them in your tasks.

Using your first workspace

For this first workspace example, you will clone a Git repository and share this repository's content to a second step to list this folder's content:

1. First, start with a new file called `clone-ls.yaml`. This file will contain a new task named `clone-and-list`:

    ```
    apiVersion: tekton.dev/v1beta1
    kind: Task
    metadata:
      name: clone-and-list
    spec:
    ```

2. To make this task as generic as possible, it will take a parameter for the repository's URL to clone. You can specify any Git repository as the `default` value:

    ```
    params:
      - name: repo
        type: string
        description: Git repository to be cloned
        default: https://github.com/joellord/handson-tekton
    ```

3. Next, you will need to define `workspaces` for this task. In this task, you will use a single workspace with the name `source`:

```
workspaces:
  - name: source
```

4. For the first step in this task, use the `alpine/git` image to clone the repository specified in the `repo` parameter. As part of the step definition, change the working directory for this container to the `source` workspace path using variable substitution:

```
steps:
  - name: clone
    image: alpine/git
    workingDir: $(workspaces.source.path)
    command:
      - /bin/sh
    args:
      - '-c'
      - git clone -v $(params.repo) ./source
```

5. For the final step, use the `alpine` image to list all the files in the current directory. As you did in the first step, specify the working directory as the workspace named `source` folder:

```
  - name: list
    image: alpine
      workingDir: $(workspaces.source.path)
    command:
      - /bin/sh
    args:
      - "-c"
      - ls ./source
```

6. Apply this task to your cluster:

```
$ kubectl apply -f ./clone-ls.yaml
```

You are now ready to start your first task that uses a workspace. Just like you did previously with other tasks, use the `tkn` CLI tool to execute this task. It will ask you a series of questions. For the `repo` parameter, you can use any GitHub repository. Next, for the name of the workspace, you will need to put in the value `source`. Accept all the default values for the other fields:

```
$ tkn task start clone-and-list
? Value for param `repo` of type `string`? https://github.com/
joellord/handson-tekton
Please give specifications for the workspace: source
? Name for the workspace : source
? Value of the Sub Path :
? Type of the Workspace : emptyDir
? Type of EmptyDir :
TaskRun started: clone-and-list-run-dtcbb
Waiting for logs to be available...
[clone] Cloning into './source'...
[clone] POST git-upload-pack (164 bytes)
[clone] POST git-upload-pack (217 bytes)
[list] README.md
...
```

If you want to start the task by specifying the CLI options, you can use the –w parameter. Specify the `name` of the workspace and the type of `volume  source` to use. In this case, it will be an `emptyDir` volume:

```
$ tkn task start clone-and-list -w name=source,emptyDir=""
--showlog
```

The output should be the same, assuming that you've used the same repository in the `repo` parameter.

In this example, Tekton created a folder to be used for the steps of this task. The first step then cloned the source code from the repository. Once this container completed its execution, the shared volume was mounted to the next container to be used by the list step. This second container was then able to use this folder to list its content.

> **Note**
>
> The `emptyDir` object is a Kubernetes-specific object. It is a volume that is created when a pod is assigned to a node and is initially empty. You can find out more about `emptyDir` at `https://kubernetes.io/docs/concepts/storage/volumes/#emptydir`.

Another way to start this task would be to write your task run directly.

Using workspaces with task runs

The previous task worked well when initiated with the `tkn` CLI tool, where you had to fill in all the information. Sometimes, you might want to have all of that information as part of a YAML file.

Unlike parameters with default values that you could use, you will need to specify the name and volume source for each workspace you have in your tasks. One way to store this information as part of your YAML files is to write a task run directly. This file will be used as a template to create your task runs. Let's see how to do this:

1. Start with a new file called `clone-and-list-tr.yaml`. In this file, create a new object of kind `TaskRun`:

    ```
    apiVersion: tekton.dev/v1beta1
    kind: TaskRun
    ```

2. In the `metadata` section of this object description, you could potentially specify a name for the task run. A unique name would mean that you would need to change the name each time you want to create a new task run, though. Instead, you will use the `generateName` field. This value is what will be prefixed to a random string to determine the name of the task run:

    ```
    metadata:
      generateName: git-clone-tr-
    ```

3. Add the `spec` field for the task run:

    ```
    spec:
    ```

4. In here, specify the values for the workspaces:

```
workspaces:
  - name: source
    emptyDir: {}
```

5. Finally, you have the choice to define your whole task using a `taskSpec` object, or you can reference an existing task with `taskRef`. Use the latter for this task run:

```
taskRef:
  name: clone-and-list
```

This time, you won't be able to apply this file to your cluster. Instead, you will need to create a new object using the `kubectl create` command. This command will make a new task run, and you will be able to see the logs using the `tkn` CLI tool:

```
$ kubectl create -f ./2-clone-and-list-tr.yaml
taskrun.tekton.dev/git-clone-tr-cqphs created
$ tkn taskrun logs git-clone-tr-cqphs
[clone] Cloning into './source'...
[clone] POST git-upload-pack (164 bytes)
[clone] POST git-upload-pack (217 bytes)
[list] README.md
...
```

This task run used `emptyDir` to store the code base from the Git repository and listed it in the next step. The volume was then deleted and can't be reused by another task or task run. If you want to share data across different tasks, you will need to use persistent volumes instead, as demonstrated in the next section.

Adding a workspace to a pipeline

So far, you've managed to share a workspace across the steps of a task. As you build some real CI/CD pipelines for your applications, you will most likely need to share some data across your pipeline tasks. A typical pipeline would start with cloning a repository, and the other tasks would perform some operations on that code base. You can do this by using a workspace at the pipeline level.

For this example, you will split the task you just created into two separate tasks. This first task clones the source code, and the entire code base is shared with the list task:

1. In a file called `split-tasks.yaml`, copy over the task from the `clone-ls.yaml` file and change the name to `clone`. You can also remove the last step as it will now be part of a new task:

```yaml
apiVersion: tekton.dev/v1beta1
kind: Task
metadata:
  name: clone
spec:
  params:
    - name: repo
      type: string
      description: Git repository to be cloned
      default: https://github.com/joellord/handson-tekton
  workspaces:
    - name: source
  steps:
    - name: clone
      image: alpine/git
      workingDir: $(workspaces.source.path)
      command:
        - /bin/sh
      args:
        - '-c'
        - git clone -v $(params.repo) ./source
```

2. Use a separator to add a second task in the same file:

```yaml
---
```

3. Create a new task called `list`. This task will have a workspace, just like the `clone` task:

```yaml
apiVersion: tekton.dev/v1beta1
kind: Task
metadata:
```

```
  name: list
spec:
  workspaces:
    - name: source
```

4. This task will have a single step. This step is the one that you removed from the original `clone-and-list` task:

```
steps:
  - name: list
    image: alpine
    workingDir: $(workspaces.source.path)
    command:
      - /bin/sh
    args:
      - "-c"
      - ls ./source
```

5. Now that you have two tasks ready, you can create a new file called `clone-and-ls-pipeline.yaml`, where you will create a new pipeline called `clone-and-list`:

```
apiVersion: tekton.dev/v1beta1
kind: Pipeline
metadata:
  name: clone-and-list
```

6. In the `spec` section of this pipeline, add a single workspace that will be used to share information across the tasks:

```
spec:
  workspaces:
    - name: codebase
```

7. Add a new task to this pipeline. This task will reference the `clone` task you've just created:

```
tasks:
  - name: clone
    taskRef:
      name: clone
```

8. To that task, add a workspace. The name of the workspace is the one in the task definition. The workspace that we assign to it is the one defined in the pipeline spec:

```
workspaces:
  - name: source
    workspace: codebase
```

9. Create a second task that references the list task. It should also have a workspace called source, which will use the codebase workspace from the pipeline. Finally, make sure that you add a runAfter object. You will only run this task after the clone task has been completed or else you will get an empty folder:

```
- name: list
  taskRef:
    name: list
  workspaces:
    - name: source
      workspace: codebase
  runAfter:
    - clone
```

10. You can apply those files and run this pipeline. For now, use an emptyDir volume for the workspace named codebase:

```
$ kubectl apply -f ./3-split-tasks.yaml
task.tekton.dev/clone created
task.tekton.dev/list created
$ kubectl apply -f ./4-clone-and-ls-pipeline.yaml
pipeline.tekton.dev/clone-and-list created
$ tkn pipeline start clone-and-list --showlog
Please give specifications for the workspace: codebase
? Name for the workspace : codebase
? Value of the Sub Path :
? Type of the Workspace : emptyDir
? Type of EmptyDir :
PipelineRun started: clone-and-list-run-x9lfd
Waiting for logs to be available...
[clone : clone] Cloning into './source'...
```

```
[clone : clone] POST git-upload-pack (164 bytes)
[clone : clone] POST git-upload-pack (217 bytes)
[list : list] ls: ./source: No such file or directory
```

At first, it might seem like something went wrong. The second task did not list the contents of the folder. The command did get executed, but the folder in which it ran was empty. That is why the `list` task didn't output the files.

The workspace was empty in the second task because we used an `emptyDir` workspace. The volume created only existed in the pod. Once the first task was completed, the pod was terminated, along with the volume. The second task used a new pod, with a new empty folder.

To share the content across tasks, you will need to use a persistent volume, which you will do in the next section.

Persisting data within a pipeline

To persist the data across your tasks, you will need to look into persistent volumes and persistent volume claims. Those are Kubernetes native objects that can be used to access some disk space on a cluster. The exact way to create a persistent volume claim in your cluster might differ from the following example. Please refer to the documentation of your cloud provider for more information. Most providers will provide you with a dynamic assignment and won't need a persistent volume.

> **Note**
>
> If you want to learn more about how `PersistentVolumes` and `PersistentVolumeClaims` work and manage them, look up the Kubernetes official documentation on the subject at `https://kubernetes.io/docs/concepts/storage/`.

For this example, I am using minikube, which requires a persistent volume that can then be claimed to be used by objects in the cluster:

1. In a new file called `persistent-volume.yaml`, create a new object of kind `PersistentVolume`. This object will have the name `tekton-pv`:

```
apiVersion: v1
kind: PersistentVolume
metadata:
```

```
   name: tekton-pv
spec:
```

2. In `spec`, you will need to specify the `storageClassName`, which is `manual` for this case. Also, add `capacity` for this persistent volume. This will allocate 2 GB of disk space for this persistent volume:

```
storageClassName: manual
capacity:
   storage: 2Gi
```

3. Next, specify all the access modes that this persistent volume will accommodate. Let's make it as flexible as possible by adding all the possible types:

```
accessModes:
  - ReadWriteMany
  - ReadWriteOnce
  - ReadOnlyMany
```

4. Finally, specify `path` where this volume is mounted on the host:

```
hostPath:
   path: "/mnt/data"
```

5. Create another file named `pvc.yaml` and add in the definition for a new Kubernetes object of type `PersistentVolumeClaim` called `tekton-pvc`:

```
apiVersion: v1
kind: PersistentVolumeClaim
metadata:
   name: tekton-pvc
spec:
```

6. The persistent volume claim for our pipeline will need the `ReadWriteMany` access mode and will require at least 1 GB of disk space:

```
accessModes:
  - ReadWriteMany
resources:
  requests:
     storage: 1Gi
```

7. Apply those two new files to your cluster:

```
$ kubectl apply -f ./persistent-volume.yaml
persistentvolume/tekton-pv created
```

```
$ kubectl apply -f ./pvc.yaml
persistentvolumeclaim/tekton-pvc created
```

You are now ready to run this pipeline and see the data being shared across all the tasks. Start the pipeline with the tkn CLI tool again, but pick pvc for the workspace type. Type tekton-pvc for the Value of Claim Name field:

```
$ tkn pipeline start clone-and-list --showlog
Please give specifications for the workspace: codebase
? Name for the workspace : codebase
? Value of the Sub Path :
? Type of the Workspace : pvc
? Value of Claim Name : tekton-pvc
PipelineRun started: clone-and-list-run-fr47q
Waiting for logs to be available...
[clone : clone] Cloning into './source'...
[clone : clone] POST git-upload-pack (164 bytes)
[clone : clone] POST git-upload-pack (217 bytes)
[list : list] README.md
...
```

This time, the list task was able to mount the volume and list the folder files. You could also specify the workspace to use as part of the CLI command by using the -w parameter:

```
$ tkn pipeline start clone-and-list --showlog -w
name=codebase,claimName=tekton-pvc
PipelineRun started: clone-and-list-run-cpbss
Waiting for logs to be available...
[clone : clone] fatal: destination path '.' already exists and
is not an empty directory.
```

You will notice that the command did not work the second time you tried it. This error is due to the nature of the persistent volume claim. Even after the pipeline was completed, the data persisted. To consistently use a single PVC, you will need to clean up your disk space once the pipeline terminates.

Cleaning up with finally

On that last pipeline run, a fatal error occurred. It tried to clone the repository, but Git requires an empty directory to clone the files into. The folder already had files from the previous clone operation.

To avoid those errors and ensure that you always start from a clean slate, you will need to clean up your persisting workspaces when the pipeline run has terminated. To do so, you will need to add a cleanup task. You will also need to ensure this task runs at the end of the pipeline, even if an error terminated the pipeline before it completed its run. This is where the `finally` tasks will come into play.

In this section, you will add a cleanup task to your pipeline that will remove all the files from the workspace:

1. Create a new file called `cleanup.yaml`. In here, create a new task named `cleanup`:

```
apiVersion: tekton.dev/v1beta1
kind: Task
metadata:
  name: cleanup
spec:
```

2. Just like the other tasks you've built in this chapter, you will need to specify a workspace for this task:

```
workspaces:
  - name: source
```

3. This task has two `steps`. The first one, called `remove-source`, uses the `rm` command to delete the folder and everything inside it. Note how you can use the variable substitution directly in the command instead of in the step definition:

```
steps:
  - name: remove-source
    image: registry.access.redhat.com/ubi8/ubi
    command:
      - /bin/bash
    args:
      - "-c"
      - "rm -rf $(workspaces.source.path)/source"
```

4. Finally, you can add a step to provide feedback to your users, telling them that the task was completed:

```
- name: message
    image: registry.access.redhat.com/ubi8/ubi
    command:
      - /bin/bash
    args:
    - "-c"
      - echo All files were deleted
```

5. Apply this file to your cluster:

```
$ kubectl apply -f ./cleanup.yaml
task.tekton.dev/cleanup configured
```

The last time you executed the pipeline, it left all those files in the /source folder. Even if we added this new task at the end of the pipeline, it still wouldn't run successfully because the folder is still not empty. You can run this task as a standalone task to clean up the folder and get ready for the next pipeline run.

Using the CLI, start the task with the workspace as a CLI argument:

```
$ tkn task start cleanup --showlog -w
name=source,claimName=tekton-pvc
TaskRun started: cleanup-run-gq8vf
Waiting for logs to be available...
[message] All files were deleted
```

You are now ready to edit your pipeline. Create a new file called clone-and-ls-and-clean.yaml and copy the content from the clone-and-ls.yaml file. In this new file, after all the tasks, add a new finally object. In there, add the cleanup task:

```
tasks:
...
finally:
  - name: clean
      taskRef:
        name: cleanup
      workspaces:
      - name: source
          workspace: codebase
```

Your pipeline is now ready to run again. Just as it did previously, it will clone the repository and list the files from it. This time, though, it will clean up everything afterward, so you have a clean persistent volume next time you want to run this pipeline:

```
$ kubectl apply -f ./clone-and-ls-and-clean.yaml
pipeline.tekton.dev/clone-and-list configured


$ tkn pipeline start clone-and-list --showlog -w
name=codebase,claimName=tekton-pvc
PipelineRun started: clone-and-list-run-vv7q9
Waiting for logs to be available...
[clone : clone] Cloning into './source'...
[clone : clone] POST git-upload-pack (164 bytes)
[clone : clone] POST git-upload-pack (217 bytes)
[list : list] README.md
...
[clean : message] All files were deleted
```

Should you rerun this task, you will not get the error message about the empty folder anymore. In this last example, you still had to specify the workspace manually in the CLI tool. Like you did with task runs, you can configure pipeline runs to use a specific persistent volume or even use a template to automate the process. You will do this in the next section.

Using workspaces in pipeline runs

As part of your pipeline definition, you cannot add a workspace the same way you could add default values to your parameters. If you want Tekton to start your pipeline automatically with the appropriate persistent volume claim, you will need to create a pipeline run:

1. Start with a new file called `pipelinerun.yaml`. In there, create an object of kind `PipelineRun`. Like what you did with task runs, this object will have a `generateName` field instead of an actual name:

```
apiVersion: tekton.dev/v1beta1
kind: PipelineRun
metadata:
  generateName: clone-and-ls-pr-
spec:
```

2. This pipeline run will use the pipeline that you just built called `clone-and-list`:

```
pipelineRef:
  name: clone-and-list
```

3. Finally, add a workspace named `codebase`. This workspace uses a persistent volume claim, and the `claimName` is `tekton-pvc`:

```
workspaces:
  - name: codebase
    persistentVolumeClaim:
      claimName: tekton-pvc
```

4. To start the `pipelinerun`, use the `kubectl create` command, and then use the `tkn` CLI tool to view the logs:

```
$ kubectl create -f ./pipelinerun.yaml
pipelinerun.tekton.dev/clone-and-ls-pr-pd94q created

$ tkn pr logs clone-and-ls-pr-pd94q -f
[clone : clone] Cloning into './source'...
[clone : clone] POST git-upload-pack (164 bytes)
[clone : clone] POST git-upload-pack (217 bytes)
[list : list] README.md
...
[clean : message] All files were deleted
```

Another exciting feature of pipeline runs is that you can use a template for those persistent volumes.

Using volume claim templates

Instead of specifying a persistent volume claim directly, you can also ask Tekton to create a temporary one for you. This can be useful when you don't need to persist data outside of your pipelines. As an additional benefit, using a volume claim template enables you to run multiple pipeline runs concurrently. To use a `volumeClaimTemplate`, you will need to write a new pipeline run. This time, you will add the `pipelineSpec`, which is a way to define your entire pipeline without relying on a separate pipeline object:

1. Start with a new file called `pvc-template.yaml`. In there, create a new `PipelineRun` object:

```
apiVersion: tekton.dev/v1beta1
```

```
kind: PipelineRun
metadata:
  generateName: clone-and-ls-pr-
```

2. In the `spec` field of the pipeline run, add a `pipelineSpec` field containing a `workspaces` list with one workspace called `codebase`:

```
spec:
  pipelineSpec:
    workspaces:
      - name: codebase
```

3. Add the tasks for this pipeline. In this example, the same two tasks that you used in the `clone-and-list` pipeline are used. However, there's no need for the `finally` task, as Tekton will destroy this volume claim once this `pipelinerun` object is removed:

```
    tasks:
      - name: clone
        taskRef:
          name: clone
        workspaces:
          - name: source
            workspace: codebase
      - name: list
        taskRef:
          name: list
        workspaces:
          - name: source
            workspace: codebase
        runAfter:
          - clone
```

4. Add the `workspaces` for this pipeline run. This is where you will specify the details of the `codebase` workspace. It will have a `volumeClaimTemplate` field, which will take a persistent volume claim definition:

```
  workspaces:
    - name: codebase
```

```
        volumeClaimTemplate:
          spec:
            accessModes:
              - ReadWriteOnce
            resources:
              requests:
                storage: 1Gi
```

5. Create a new pipeline run using `kubectl`:

```
$ kubectl create -f ./pvc-template.yaml
pipelinerun.tekton.dev/clone-and-ls-pr-smkxt created

$ tkn pr logs -f clone-and-ls-pr-smkxt
[clone : clone] Cloning into './source'...
[clone : clone] POST git-upload-pack (164 bytes)
[clone : clone] POST git-upload-pack (217 bytes)
[list : list] README.md
...
```

If you run this kubectl create command again, you will not get an error message about Git needing an empty directory. This volume claim template creates a new PVC for each pipeline execution. You now have all the required information about workspaces to start with the exercises.

Getting your hands dirty

Data sharing across tasks and pipelines should have no secrets for you now. You are ready to test your knowledge with the following exercises. In order to complete those challenges, you will need to use the concepts introduced here, along with notions from the previous chapters. The solutions to these exercises can be found in the *Assessments* section at the end of the book.

Write and read

Create a task that uses a workspace to share information across its two steps. The first step will write a message, specified in a parameter, to a file in the workspace. The second step will output the content of the file in the logs. Try running the task using the `-w` parameter in the `tkn` CLI tool.

> **Tips**
>
> - Use the variable substitutions to get the path of the workspace and append a file name.
>
> - Use the `cat` command to output the content of a file.
>
> - You can use an `emptyDir` volume when the data is shared within a task.

Pick a card

Using the Deck of Cards API available at `http://deckofcardsapi.com/`, create a pipeline that would generate a new deck of cards and then pick a single card from it. The first call will generate a deck ID that you can then use in the next task to pick a card. Output the card value and suit in the second task.

> **Tips**
>
> - Use `https://deckofcardsapi.com/api/deck/new/shuffle/` to create a new deck of cards and `https://deckofcardsapi.com/api/deck/<deck_id>/draw/` to draw a card. The value for `<deck_id>` is found in the first call.
>
> - You can use a Node.js or a jq image to manipulate the JSON objects.
>
> - Use a workspace to share the deck ID across the tasks.

Hello admin

Build a pipeline that will return a different greeting, whether the username passed as a parameter is *"admin"* or something else. This pipeline should have two tasks. The first task will verify the username and output the role (admin or user) in the result. The second task will pick up this role and display the appropriate message from a ConfigMap mounted as a workspace.

> **Tips**
>
> - Don't forget to use the `runAfter` list for the second task, or else you won't have access to the results.
>
> - When using a ConfigMap as a workspace, each key-value pair from the data collection is stored as a file in the mounted folder.
>
> - Since the first task gave you a role, use key-value pairs in the `$ROLE-messageId` format for your ConfigMap.

Summary

You now know how to persist data and use shared volumes across various tasks in a Tekton pipeline. Now that you can share information such as code bases or images, it will be easier to make examples closer to your day-to-day life as a software developer and CI/CD author.

You've also seen how you can build task runs and pipeline runs directly and pass them arguments such as the parameter values or the workspace definition.

If you've done the exercises, more specifically the last one, you had to use some `if` statements in your Bash scripts to validate the user role. In Tekton, there is a way to perform some tasks based on specific conditions instead of relying on Bash scripting. These are called **when expressions** and will be introduced in the next chapter.

8
Adding when Expressions

In the pipelines you've built so far, Tekton executed tasks in a specified order as long as the previous one was successful. As you work your way toward more advanced CI/CD Tekton pipelines, you will encounter cases where some of your tasks will need to be guarded. A typical use case would be to prevent a deployment task from being executed if the branch on which a commit happened is anything but `main`.

When expressions can be added to Tekton tasks to add a condition on when to execute a specific task. In this chapter, you will learn more about building your `when` expressions and how to add them to a task to block their execution.

Finally, to decide whether a task should be executed or not, you will see how you can use pipeline parameters as an input to evaluate.

In this chapter, we are going to cover the following main topics:

- Introducing when expressions
- Using when expressions with parameters
- Using the notin operator
- Using when expressions with results

Technical requirements

You can find all of the examples described in this chapter in the `chapter-8` folder of the Git repository: `https://github.com/PacktPublishing/Building-CI-CD-systems-using-Tekton`.

You can also see the Code in Action videos at the following link: `https://bit.ly/3rBiQ2R`

Introducing when expressions

Sometimes, you will want some tasks to happen based on certain conditions. To do this, you will need to use when expressions. You can think of them as `if` statements for your pipelines.

Tekton evaluates when expressions before task execution. If the described condition is met, Tekton will proceed with the task. Otherwise, the task is skipped.

When you need when expressions, you will add them as part of the task definition in a pipeline description.

They have three properties – `input`, `operator`, and `values`. This is what a typical when expression would look like:

```
when:
  - input: "true"
    operator: in
    values: ["true"]
```

For `input`, you can use a static string or a variable substitution. Typical variables would be a pipeline parameter value or the value of a previous task result.

There are two operators that you can use to perform the comparison – `in` or `notin`. As the name suggests, they validate whether a value is in or not in the array of values provided.

Finally, you need to add an array of strings representing `values` to be compared with `input`. Just like `input`, `values` could be pipeline parameters or results from previous tasks. It could also be set to the bound state of a workspace, indicating whether an optional workspace is present or not.

Now that you know how to compose a when expression, you can add one to your CI/CD pipelines.

Using when expressions with parameters

For this first example, you will build a guess-the-number type of game. When you start the pipeline, it will ask you for a number as a parameter. In the pipeline, a when expression will be used to compare this parameter's value with a hardcoded number. If the number is a match, it will output a message saying that you guessed the number accurately. The logger task that you built in *Chapter 5*, *Jumping into Pipelines*, will be used in this pipeline to output the messages. For convenience, here is the task definition:

```
apiVersion: tekton.dev/v1beta1
kind: Task
metadata:
  name: logger
spec:
  params:
    - name: text
      type: string
  steps:
    - name: log
      image: registry.access.redhat.com/ubi8/ubi-minimal
      script: |
        DATE=$(date +%d/%m/%Y\ %T)
        echo [$DATE] - $(params.text)
```

Once this task has been applied to your cluster, you can start building your pipeline using the following steps:

1. First, in a new file named guess.yaml, add the basic definition to create a pipeline called guess-game:

    ```
    apiVersion: tekton.dev/v1beta1
    kind: Pipeline
    metadata:
      name: guess-game
    spec:
    ```

2. This pipeline will take one parameter. number is what will be compared in the when expression to display the message to the user. This parameter is called number and is of the string type. You can add an optional description:

```
params:
  - name: number
    description: Pick a number
    type: string
```

3. The pipeline will have a single task in it. This task will display a message saying You win!. To do so, add a new task called win that will reference the logger task. Add the You win value to the parameter called text:

```
  - name: win
    params:
      - name: text
        value: You win
    taskRef:
      name: logger
```

Should you run this pipeline as it is right now, it will display the message every time. For this example, though, it should only be logged if the parameter called number has the value "3". To prevent this task from running for any other value, a when expression can be added.

4. Add a when field to the task. For input, use $(params.number), the pipeline parameter called number whose value will be entered when you start the pipeline with the CLI tool. The operator value to use here is in, and the list of possible values is limited to a single one, the number 3:

```
      when:
        - input: $(params.number)
          operator: in
          values: ["3"]
```

5. Apply this new pipeline to your cluster:

```
$ kubectl apply -f ./guess.yaml
pipeline.tekton.dev/guess-game created
```

You are now ready to test out this pipeline. First, provide the value 3 for the parameter:

```
$ tkn pipeline start guess-game --showlog
? Value for param `number` of type `string`? 3
PipelineRun started: guess-game-run-vxjwl
Waiting for logs to be available...
[win : log] [02/04/2021 14:03:39] - You win
```

You guessed the number, and a message indicating that you won was displayed. If you try with another value, such as 1, nothing should be shown in the console:

```
$ tkn pipeline start guess-game --showlog
? Value for param `number` of type `string`? 1
PipelineRun started: guess-game-run-nblg2
Waiting for logs to be available...
```

Since the condition specified in the when expression was not met, Tekton never executed the task; hence, nothing was outputted. In the next section, you will see how you could add some outputs when the value does not match the number 3.

Using the notin operator

In the previous example, you blocked a task execution by using a when expression. Sometimes, you might want to perform another task if a value is not matched. By using the notin operator, you can add what would be similar to an else statement. For this following example, you will add a You lose message when the number is not 3:

1. Copy over the pipeline from game.yaml into a new file called guess-notin. yaml. Change the name of this new pipeline to guess-game-notin, and keep everything else:

```yaml
apiVersion: tekton.dev/v1beta1
kind: Pipeline
metadata:
  name: guess-game-notin
spec:
  params:
  ...
    tasks:
```

```
    - name: win
  ...
```

2. At the end of this pipeline, add a new task called `lose`. This task object will reference the same `logger` task. As a parameter, it will take `You lose` as the value for `text`:

```
    - name: lose
      params:
        - name: text
          value: You lose
      taskRef:
        name: logger
```

3. Add a `when` expression to this task. You will use the same values for the `input` and `values` fields for this expression, but this time, the `operator` value will be `notin`:

```
      when:
        - input: $(params.number)
          operator: notin
          values: ["3"]
```

4. Apply this file to your cluster and rerun the following pipeline:

```
$ kubectl apply -f ./guess-notin.yaml
pipeline.tekton.dev/guess-game-notin created

$ tkn pipeline start guess-game-notin --showlog
? Value for param `number` of type `string`? 3
PipelineRun started: guess-game-notin-run-nxrpm
Waiting for logs to be available...
[win : log] [02/04/2021 14:20:30] - You win

$ tkn pipeline start guess-game-notin --showlog
? Value for param `number` of type `string`? 1
PipelineRun started: guess-game-notin-run-6zvbl
Waiting for logs to be available...
[lose : log] [02/04/2021 14:20:45] - You lose
```

In addition to the winning message when the parameter value is 3, you can now also see the lost message when you use any other value as the parameter. In this case, you used parameters for the input, but you could just as easily use $(tasks.<task-name>. results.<result-name>) to substitute a result value from a previous task.

Using when expressions with results

A common use case when dealing with pipelines is to block the execution of certain tasks based on the outcome of an earlier task. In order to achieve that, you would need to use a result. This is what you will do in this section.

First, you will create a new task that will generate a random number. Then, you will use a pipeline similar to the one you've used so far in this chapter. The decision to run the win or lose task will depend on the resulting random number from the first task:

1. In a new file called guess-result.yaml, create the following task that uses a **Universal Base Image (UBI)** to generate a random number and store it as a result:

```
apiVersion: tekton.dev/v1beta1
kind: Task
metadata:
  name: random-number-generator
spec:
  results:
    - name: random-number
      description: random number
  steps:
    - name: generate-number
      image: registry.access.redhat.com/ubi8/ubi-minimal
      script: |
        NUMBER=$((1 + $RANDOM % 3))
        echo Random number picked, result is $NUMBER
        echo $NUMBER > $(results.random-number.path)
---
```

2. In the same file, following the - - - separator, create a new pipeline named guess-result:

```
apiVersion: tekton.dev/v1beta1
kind: Pipeline
```

```
metadata:
  name: guess-result
spec:
  tasks:
```

3. For the first task, use the `random-number-generator` task:

```
- name: generate
  taskRef:
    name: random-number-generator
```

4. Next, add your `win` task. This task should only be triggered when the result from the first task is the number 3. Don't forget to add a `runAfter` field to ensure that this task runs after the number was generated and the result was stored:

```
- name: win
  params:
    - name: text
      value: You win
  taskRef:
    name: logger
  when:
    - input: $(tasks.generate.results.random-number)
      operator: in
      values: ["3"]
  runAfter:
    - generate
```

5. Finally, add a `lose` task that will output the text `You lose` if the random number is not the number 3:

```
- name: lose
  params:
    - name: text
      value: You lose
  taskRef:
    name: logger
  when:
    - input: $(tasks.generate.results.random-number)
```

```
          operator: notin
          values: ["3"]
    runAfter:
      - generate
```

6. Apply this file and run this new pipeline:

```
$ kubectl apply -f ./guess-result.yaml
task.tekton.dev/random-number-generator created
pipeline.tekton.dev/guess-result created

$ tkn pipeline start guess-result --showlog
PipelineRun started: guess-result-run-f4c2j
Waiting for logs to be available...
[generate : generate-number] Random number picked, result
is 3
[win : log] [20/05/2021 12:04:14] - You win
```

As you can see, only the task matching the when expression was executed while the other one was ignored. This type of pattern would be used in your pipelines whenever you need a condition to decide whether to execute a task or not. You make sure that the first task returns a result and then use that result to decide whether to run the task or not.

Getting your hands dirty

You can now block tasks from being executed depending on some values found in parameters or results. You are ready to test your knowledge with the following exercises. To complete the challenges, you will need to use the concepts introduced here and notions from the previous chapters.

As usual, you can find the solutions to these exercises at the end of this book, in the *Assessment* section.

Hello Admin

Build a pipeline that will take a username as a parameter. If the username is admin, log the text Hello Admin. For any other username, output a simple Hello message.

> **Tips**
>
> - This exercise is similar to the example you just did.
>
> - Use the `logger` task to output messages.
>
> - You will need two tasks, each with a different when expression.

Critical Hit

In role-playing games using dice, rolling a 20 on a 20-sided die is sometimes referred to as rolling a critical hit. For this exercise, build a pipeline that would log `Critical Hit` when the result of a dice roll is `20`. To do so, use a task that will generate a random number between 1 and 20 and produce a result that the when expression of a second task can pick up.

> **Tips**
>
> - You built a task that generates a random number in *Chapter 5, Jumping into Pipelines*; try reusing it.
>
> - You can use the `logger` task to output messages.
>
> - Don't forget to add a `runAfter` property to the task that uses the dice roll task results.

Not working on weekends

Even your servers deserve a break. Build a pipeline with a task that Tekton will only execute on weekdays. The task should log the message `Working` to simulate some work.

> **Tips**
>
> - You will need a task to get the day of the week with the Linux `date +%w` command.
>
> - If the command doesn't work at first, it might be due to a trailing line break. Try using `date +%w | tr -d' \n'`.
>
> - Don't forget to use `runAfter` to enforce the order in which the tasks will run.

Summary

In this chapter, you've seen how to use conditional statements in your pipelines. You saw how you could use a parameter to block a task if needed. You can also use a result from a previous task to do the same thing.

You now have all the necessary components to build very powerful flows that will make you deploy your applications faster and more reliably.

To deploy your application into a real server, you will need to provide it with some credentials. Those can't be stored in a YAML file pushed to your repository; you will need to keep them a secret. This will be addressed in the next chapter.

9
Securing Authentication

Once you start building pipelines to be used in your enterprise, there is a good chance that you will use them on a private Git repository as opposed to a public one. The same is most likely true for your image registry. To access those resources, you will need to authenticate to the servers hosting them. To do so, you will use secrets.

In this chapter, you will learn about how Tekton handles authentication. Then, you will see how you can clone a private repository in a task. Finally, you will learn how to use stored images on a private registry for steps in your Tekton tasks.

In this chapter, we are going to cover the following main topics:

- Introducing authentication in Tekton
- Authenticating into a Git repository
- Authenticating into a container registry

Technical requirements

For the examples in this chapter, you will need access to a private Git repository, along with the credentials to access it. GitHub can provide you with unlimited private repositories. You might need a paid tier with Docker Hub to create a private image for your image registry.

You can find all of the examples described in this chapter in the `chapter-9` folder of the Git repository: `https://github.com/PacktPublishing/Building-CI-CD-systems-using-Tekton`.

You can also see the Code in Action videos at: `https://bit.ly/3y5lTCQ`

Introducing authentication in Tekton

So far, you've used publicly available Git repositories and Docker registries. It works well in theory, but you will probably need to authenticate to those servers in practice. Tekton has some built-in mechanisms in place to help you with this.

The support for authentication in Tekton is done through the Kubernetes first-class object secrets. These secrets will be used by a service account specified in the task definition.

For Tekton to use these secrets, it will need to have some specific annotations. Tekton will convert secrets with the necessary annotations in the authentication files required by either Git or Docker.

Authenticating into a Git repository

For this first hands-on example, you will start by creating a private repository in GitHub. Once this Git repository is ready, you will create a Secret object in Kubernetes. This object will contain your credentials and will be assigned to a service account. Using this specific service account in your runs, you will be able to clone a private repository.

For the following examples, you will need a private GitHub repository with a `README.md` file and the credentials for it.

Once you have a private repository in place, you can create the following task in a file named `task.yaml`. This task will use the `alpine/git` image to clone a repository and output the content of the `README.md` file:

```
apiVersion: tekton.dev/v1beta1
kind: Task
```

```
metadata:
 name: read-file
spec:
 params:
   - name: private-repo
     type: string
 steps:
   - name: clone
     image: alpine/git
     script: |
         mkdir /temp && cd /temp
         git clone $(params.private-repo) .
         cat README.md
```

Make sure that you apply this file to your cluster using the following command:

```
$ kubectl apply -f ./task.yaml
task.tekton.dev/read-file created
```

In the following two examples, you will see how to use basic authentication (username and password) and **Secure Shell** (**SSH**) authentication in conjunction with this task to access a private repository on GitHub.

Basic authentication

GitHub won't let you authenticate using your username and password directly. Instead, you will need to create a token that can then be used as your password. This token can be easily revoked if you accidentally publish it somewhere.

To learn how to create a token, you can look at the GitHub documentation at `https://docs.github.com/en/github/authenticating-to-github/creating-a-personal-access-token`.

Once you have your token, you will be ready to create a secret to clone your repository:

1. Create a new file called `secret.yaml` and add a new object of kind `Secret`:

    ```
    apiVersion: v1
    kind: Secret
    ```

2. In the `metadata` section, you can name your object `git-basic-auth`. You will also need to provide some annotations to indicate to Tekton when it should use these credentials. In this case, Tekton will use these credentials with `github.com`:

```
metadata:
  name: git-basic-auth
  annotations:
    tekton.dev/git-0: https://github.com
```

3. Specify the `type` of secret in the `type` property. This will be a Kubernetes native `basic-auth` type:

```
type: kubernetes.io/basic-auth
```

4. Finally, add your credentials. In the `stringData` object, add your username and use the token you just created as your password:

```
stringData:
  username: joellord
  password: <secret token>
```

5. Apply this file to your cluster:

```
$ kubectl apply -f ./secret.yaml
secret/git-basic-auth created
```

You now have a set of credentials that Tekton can use to access your private repository. To use these credentials, you will need to create a **ServiceAccount** that will then be associated with your runs:

1. Start in a new file called `serviceaccount.yaml`. Create an object of kind `ServiceAccount`:

```
apiVersion: v1
kind: ServiceAccount
```

2. In the `metadata` section, you can name this object `git-auth-sa`:

```
metadata:
  name: git-auth-sa
```

3. List the `secrets` to which this service account will have access. There is a single element to the array, which is the newly created secret called `git-basic-auth`:

```
secrets:
 - name: git-basic-auth
```

4. Apply this new file to your cluster:

```
$ kubectl apply -f ./serviceaccount.yaml
serviceaccount/git-auth-sa created
```

You now have everything needed to access your private code repository. To bind all of these objects together, you will need to create a task run. This run will associate the parameter values and the service account to use with the task described at the beginning of this chapter:

1. In a new file named `taskrun.yaml`, create a new `TaskRun` object. This task run won't have a specific name but will use the `generateName` property to generate a unique name that starts with `git-auth-`:

```
apiVersion: tekton.dev/v1beta1
kind: TaskRun
metadata:
  generateName: git-auth-
```

2. In the `spec` section of your file, specify the service account to use. In this case, it will be the `git-auth-sa` account:

```
spec:
    serviceAccountName: git-auth-sa
```

3. Also, specify a value for the `private-repo` parameter. This value should be a private repository hosted on GitHub:

```
params:
  - name: private-repo
    value: https://github.com/joellord/secret-repo.git
```

4. Finally, tell Tekton which task to use with this run. Use the `read-file` task that you created earlier:

```
taskRef:
  name: read-file
```

5. Create a new task run using the `kubectl` command and use the `tkn` CLI tool to see the logs:

```
$ kubectl create -f ./taskrun.yaml
taskrun.tekton.dev/git-auth-kgp91 created


$ tkn taskrun logs git-auth-kgp91
[clone] Cloning into '.'...
[clone] Shhh... This is a secret repository.
```

You should see the content of the README.md file in your private repository as part of the task run logs.

You are now able to use your username and password to log into a Git repository and clone your repository. However, you might be used to using SSH authentication when dealing with GitHub. The next section will show you how to do so.

SSH authentication

While basic authentication can be helpful in some instances, when working with a team on a shared repository, chances are you will be using SSH authentication to connect to your repository.

In this section, you will see how you can change the last secret and service account to now use SSH-based authentication:

1. Start by creating a new file called `secret-ssh.yaml`. This file will contain a new secret named `git-ssh-auth`:

```
apiVersion: v1
kind: Secret
metadata:
  name: git-ssh-auth
```

2. Add the `annotations` section so that Tekton knows with which domain these credentials are to be used. Note that you will need to omit the protocol and use only the domain name in this case:

```
annotations:
    tekton.dev/git-0: github.com
```

3. The `type` of secret will be `kubernetes.io/ssh-auth`:

```
type: kubernetes.io/ssh-auth
```

4. Next, you will need to provide your SSH key and add it to the `ssh-privatekey` property of the `stringData` object:

```
stringData:
  ssh-privatekey: |
    -----BEGIN OPENSSH PRIVATE KEY-----
    B3BlbnNzaC...
     NhAAAA...
    -----END OPENSSH PRIVATE KEY-----
```

> **Note**
>
> Assuming that you've already used `git` with SSH authentication, you can find your SSH key in your home folder, in a file called `id_rsa` in the `.ssh` folder. You can see it in your terminal by typing `cat ~/.ssh/id_rsa`.

5. Next, you will need to add `github.com` as a trusted domain in the `known_hosts` property:

```
    known_hosts: github.com,140.82.112.4 ssh-rsa
AAAAB3NzaC1yc2EAAAABIwAAAQEAq2A7hRGmdnm9tUDbO9IDSwBK6
TbQa+PXYPCPy6rbTrTtw7PHkccKrpp0yVhp5HdEIcKr6pLlVDBfOL
X9QUsyCOV0wzfjIJNlGEYsdlLJizHhbn2mUjvSAHQqZETYP81eFz
LQNnPHt4EVVUh7VfDESU84KezmD5QlWpXLmvU31/yMf+Se8xhHT
vKSCZIFImWwoG6mbUoWf9nzpIoaSjB+weqqUUmpaaasXVal72J+
UX2B+2RPW3RcT0eOzQgqlJL3RKrTJvdsjE3JEAvGq3lGHSZXy28G3
skua2SmVi/w4yCE6gbODqnTWlg7+wC604ydGXA8VJiS5ap43
JXiUFFAaQ==
```

> **Note**
>
> You can find the known host entry in the `known_hosts` file in the `.ssh` folder of your home directory if you've already used `git` with SSH authentication. You only need the entry for `github.com`. You can find this entry in your terminal using the `cat ~/.ssh/known_hosts | grep github.com` command.

6. You can also create a new file called `serviceaccount-ssh.yaml`, in which you will create a new service account named `git-auth-sa`. This new object will use the `git-ssh-auth` secret you just made:

```
apiVersion: v1
kind: ServiceAccount
metadata:
  name: git-auth-sa
secrets:
  - name: git-ssh-auth
```

7. Copy over the content from `task.yaml` in a new file called `task-ssh.yaml`. Change the script part to add the two following lines:

```
script: |
    cd /root && mkdir .ssh && cd .ssh
    cp ~/.ssh/* .
    mkdir /temp && cd /temp
    git clone $(params.private-repo) .
    cat README.md
```

> **Note**
>
> These two additional lines are required to get the SSH tool to work in the container. This is due to how SSH looks for those files and how Tekton mounts the home folder. You can find out more about this issue in the Tekton documentation at `https://tekton.dev/docs/pipelines/auth/#using-ssh-authentication-in-git-type-tasks`.

8. Apply these files to your Kubernetes cluster:

```
$ kubectl apply -f ./secret-ssh.yaml
secret/git-ssh-auth created

$ kubectl apply -f ./serviceaccount-ssh.yaml
serviceaccount/git-auth-sa configured

$ kubectl apply -f ./task-ssh.yaml
task.tekton.dev/read-file configured
```

9. In your `taskrun.yaml` file, change the `private-repo` parameter to use the SSH URL for the repository:

```
params:
  - name: private-repo
    value: git@github.com:joellord/secret-repo
```

10. You can now create a new task run with the `kubectl` CLI tool, and see the output with the `tkn` tool:

```
$ kubectl create -f ./taskrun-ssh.yaml
taskrun.tekton.dev/git-auth-grzw4 created


$ tkn taskrun logs -f git-auth-grzw4
[clone] Cloning into '.'...
[clone] Shhh... This is a secret repository.
```

You can see that the code is cloned from the private repository, and the content of the `README.md` file is seen in the logs of the task run that you created. Often, in your projects, you will also need to use a private image registry; this will be introduced in the next section.

Authenticating in a container registry

If the image you need for a task is located in a private registry, you can use an image pull secret to add your credentials to the service account that downloads the images.

To do so, you first need to create a set of credentials in your Kubernetes cluster. You can do this with the `kubectl` CLI tool with the following command to create an object of kind `Secret` called `registry-creds`:

```
$ kubectl create secret docker-registry registry-creds
--docker-server=<server> --docker-username=<username> --docker-
password=<password> --docker-email=<email>
```

> **Note**
>
> Here, replace `server`, `username`, `password`, and `email` with the matching values for your registry.

Next, you will need to create a new service account for your cluster. You can do this using the following YAML. This service account, called `authenticated`, will use the newly created `registry-creds` to authenticate to the image registry. You can name this file `registry-sa.yaml`:

```
apiVersion: v1
kind: ServiceAccount
metadata:
 name: authenticated
secrets:
 - name: registry-creds
imagePullSecrets:
 - name: registry-creds
```

Create a new task called `private` in a file named `private.yaml`. In this case, I am using the private image called `joellord/private`, located in my Docker Hub registry. You will need to change this to a private image to which you have access:

```
apiVersion: tekton.dev/v1beta1
kind: Task
metadata:
 name: private
spec:
 steps:
  - image: joellord/private
    command:
     - /bin/sh
     - -c
     - echo hello
```

After you've added this service account to your cluster, you can use it with the Tekton command-line tool when you need to authenticate to a registry to download an image. To do so, you can use the `-s` parameter with `tkn`:

```
$ kubectl apply -f ./registry-sa.yaml
serviceaccount/authenticated created


$ kubectl apply -f ./private.yaml
task.tekton.dev/private created
```

```
$ tkn task start private --showlog -s authenticated
```

This command will start the task, and this time, it will use the service account with access to your credentials to authenticate to the image registry.

Summary

In this chapter, you've learned how to authenticate to a Git repository or an image registry. Now that you know how to do so, Tekton will be allowed to download your team's source code or images.

You have seen how you can use Kubernetes secrets to authenticate to those servers. For the Git examples, you've learned that you can either use a username/password authentication or an SSH-based authentication mechanism. Those principles can also apply to image registries.

Finally, you've seen how you can use the kubectl command-line tool to build a secret to use with your Tekton pipelines to access a private registry. You then saw how the tkn CLI tool could link the service account to a task to create an authenticated task run.

You now have all the necessary knowledge to build your complete CI/CD pipelines with Tekton. The only missing piece will be to trigger your pipelines automatically. This functionality will require the help of a sister project of Tekton, which is Tekton Triggers. Triggers is the subject of the next part of this book.

Section 3: Tekton Triggers

To take the CI/CD automation one step further, it is possible to add Tekton Triggers as part of the Kubernetes cluster. Tekton Triggers is a sister project of Tekton Pipelines that lets you automatically start Pipelines based on actions in a code repository such as a commit to the master branch.

In this section, you will start by installing all the necessary tools to enable Tekton Triggers. Once this tooling is ready to be used, you will also need to configure your server and Git repository to enable your new triggers.

Once this configuration is completed, you will tackle some hands-on examples on how to create a trigger inside your cluster and how to configure your Git repository to send the webhooks that will start the pipeline.

By the end of this section, you will have an understanding of how Tekton Triggers works and where it fits in your CI/CD systems.

The following chapters are included in this section:

- *Chapter 10, Getting Started with Triggers*
- *Chapter 11, Triggering Tekton*

10
Getting Started with Triggers

So far, you've learned how to create flexible and powerful pipelines using Tekton. Each time you wanted to start one of those pipelines, you had to use the `tkn` CLI tool to generate the pipeline run. If you remember from *Chapter 1, A Brief History of CI/CD*, the ultimate goal of CI/CD is to automate these processes.

In this chapter, you will learn about **Tekton Triggers**. Triggers is a sister project of Tekton Pipelines that introduces new custom resources to automate your CI/CD pipelines further. Using Triggers, you will learn how to start your pipelines using webhooks automatically. Since Tekton Triggers is an independent project, you will need to start by installing those new objects and configure your cluster to accept incoming requests. Once your cluster is ready to accept incoming webhooks, you will learn about the basic objects that will enable you to create Tekton Triggers to automate your CI/CD pipelines.

In this chapter, we are going to cover the following main topics:

- Introducing Tekton Triggers
- Installing Tekton Triggers
- Configuring your cluster
- Defining new objects

Technical requirements

Check out the following link to see the Code in Action video: `https://bit.ly/3ya1v3I`

Introducing Tekton Triggers

In *Chapter 1*, *A Brief History of CI/CD*, you saw how continuous deployment refers to automatically deploying an application when changes are made to the code. So far, in all the Tekton examples you've seen, you had to trigger the pipeline for it to start manually. It is now time to bring the automation processes one step further and automatically start those pipelines as soon as some changes are pushed to your code repository.

To do so, you will use another tool called Tekton Triggers. Triggers enables you to accept incoming webhooks to your cluster and take appropriate action based on the content of these requests.

Using trigger templates, trigger bindings, and event listeners, three new objects in your Kubernetes cluster, you will be able to manipulate incoming HTTP requests, map the data into parameters, and then pass those values to your pipelines.

This process will trigger your pipeline, which would ultimately automatically deploy your application into your cluster.

Before we dig into how to use Tekton Triggers, let's start by installing it on your cluster.

Installing Tekton Triggers

Installing Tekton Triggers is very similar to Tekton Pipelines installation. You can use the `kubectl` command to apply the YAML files that are provided in the GitHub repository. You can find the most recent details of the installation, along with the URLs to the latest files on the Tekton website at `https://tekton.dev/docs/triggers/install/`.

The installation is in two steps. First, install the trigger **custom resource definitions** (**CRDs**) by running the following command:

```
$ kubectl apply -f https://storage.googleapis.com/tekton-releases/triggers/latest/release.yaml
```

Next, you will need to install the **interceptors**. An interceptor is an object that contains the logic necessary to validate and filter webhooks coming from various sources. The Tekton Triggers team provides you with four basic interceptors (GitHub, Gitlab, Bitbucket, and **Common Expression Language (CEL)**). To install them, you can use the following command:

```
$ kubectl apply -f https://storage.googleapis.com/tekton-
releases/triggers/latest/interceptors.yaml
```

You now have everything needed to use Tekton Triggers. You can validate your installation by running the `tkn version` command, which will now list the version of Tekton Triggers in addition to the version of the CLI and Pipelines:

```
$ tkn version
Client version: 0.17.1
Pipeline version: v0.23.0
Triggers version: v0.13.0
Dashboard version: v0.16.1
```

The last thing you will need is to create the necessary service account for the Tekton triggers. For the examples of this book, you can use the same `rbac.yaml` file that is used in the Tekton documentation:

```
$ kubectl apply -f https://raw.githubusercontent.com/tektoncd/
triggers/main/examples/rbac.yaml
```

To find out more about this file and why it is necessary to start your triggers, you can look at the documentation at `https://tekton.dev/docs/triggers/ eventlisteners/#serviceaccountname`.

Now that Triggers is installed, you will be able to listen for events from GitHub, but for the webhooks to reach your cluster, you will need to expose a route to the outside world. This will be done in the next section.

Configuring your cluster

In order for external services, such as GitHub, to connect to your triggers, you will need to expose a service to the outside world. This process varies a lot depending on the type of cluster that you are using. Should you be using minikube, the process will be relatively simple. For cloud-based solutions, the setup might vary from one cloud provider to another, and you might need to read up the documentation from your specific supplier.

Using a local cluster

If you are using a local version on your computer, such as minikube, you will need additional software to help you expose your event listeners.

Right now, there is no way for GitHub to find your personal computer when it triggers a webhook. To do so, you will need a tool called **ngrok** to create a tunnel between your laptop and the outside world.

To install ngrok, go to `https://ngrok.com/download`. From there, follow the instructions on the page to install it on your computer, as shown in the following screenshot:

Figure 10.1 – The ngrok download page

The specifics of how to use this tool will be shown in the next chapter, when you will need to use it to expose your event listeners.

Cloud-based clusters

If you are running an instance of Kubernetes in the cloud, you will need to use an ingress to expose the service created by Tekton Triggers. The following instructions have been tested on GKE version `1.13.7-gke.24` according to the documentation found at `https://tekton.dev/docs/triggers/exposing-eventlisteners/`.

The essential part is the installation of the nginx ingress controller. You can find the appropriate command for your cloud environment at `https://kubernetes.github.io/ingress-nginx/deploy/`. If you are using GKE, the exact command to install the ingress controller is as follows:

```
$ kubectl apply -f https://raw.githubusercontent.com/
```

```
kubernetes/ingress-nginx/controller-v0.34.1/deploy/static/
provider/cloud/deploy.yaml
```

Once you have the ingress controller installed on your cluster, you will be able to expose services to the outside world. In this specific case, you will want to expose your event listener service. You most likely don't have one yet. Creating your first event listener will be done in *Chapter 11, Triggering Tekton*.

Once you do have your first event listener in place, though, you will need to find out the name for this service. This should be `el-<YOUR_EVENTLISTENER_NAME>`. To find the exact name of the service, you can run the following command:

```
$ kubectl get services
NAME          TYPE        CLUSTER-IP      EXTERNAL-IP    PORT(S)
AGE

el-listener   ClusterIP   10.108.23.37    <none>         8080/TCP
8d

kubernetes    ClusterIP   10.96.0.1       <none>         443/TCP
9d
```

Once you have found the name for your event listener service (`el-listener` in my case), note it down, as you will need it in your ingress definition.

The actual definition of your ingress resource will vary based on the cloud provider that you are using. Be sure to check out the appropriate documentation for your provider. The following example should be working for GKE. Be sure to change the `serviceName` field to the actual name of your event listener service:

```
apiVersion: extensions/v1beta1
kind: Ingress
metadata:
  name: el-ingress
  annotations:
    kubernetes.io/ingress.class: nginx
    nginx.ingress.kubernetes.io/ssl-redirect: "false"
spec:
  rules:
    - http:
        paths:
          - path: /
            backend:
```

```
                    serviceName: <YOUR_EVENTLISTENER_NAME>
                    servicePort: 8080
```

Once you have this ingress applied in your cluster, you will be able to get the public address of this service by using the following command:

```
$ kubectl get ingress el-ingress
```

Use the value from the address field with a `curl` command and you will be able to reach the event listener.

Now that you've installed Tekton Triggers, it is time to dig into what this installation brings to your cluster and how you can use Triggers to further automate your CI/CD pipelines.

Defining new objects

Once you install Tekton Triggers into your cluster, you will have access to three new objects. These objects will then be used to create your triggers and automate your pipeline's final part. The following figure describes the flow that happens when a trigger is started:

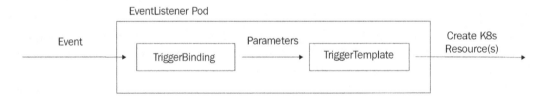

Figure 10.2 – Tekton trigger flow

In this section, you will learn more about each of these components.

Trigger templates

A **TriggerTemplate** is a new primitive that will be available to you once you've installed Tekton Triggers. The main goal of the trigger template is to be a template for the resources that the trigger will create.

Trigger templates are to Tekton triggers what pipelines are to pipeline runs. While the templates don't do any work, they describe what pipeline should be triggered and the parameters to pass to that pipeline.

Parameters for the trigger templates are similarly passed to the object, as is the case with pipelines and tasks. They have a name, an optional description, and an optional default value. You can then access those parameters using variable substitution by using $(tt. params.<name>).

A typical trigger template is described in a YAML file, as follows:

```
apiVersion: triggers.tekton.dev/v1alpha1
kind: TriggerTemplate
metadata:
  name: template-name
spec:
  params:
    ...
  resourcetemplates:
    ...
```

The parameters are added to the params list. The resourcetemplates list describes the pipeline run that will be created when the trigger is launched.

Trigger bindings

The **TriggerBinding** object takes the information from the incoming requests provided by the event listener object and transforms it for consumption by the trigger template. Its purpose is to capture some fields and store them as parameters.

The reasoning behind having a separate trigger template and trigger binding is to promote reusability across your pipelines and triggers. For example, most of your bindings for GitHub hooks will extract similar information to pass it to your templates. On the other hand, the template for each specific repository will most likely be a different one for each pipeline. By creating one generic binding, you can reuse it across all of your projects.

The YAML description of your trigger bindings would go as follows:

```
apiVersion: triggers.tekton.dev/v1alpha1
kind: TriggerBinding
metadata:
  name: binding-name
spec:
  params:
```

```
- name: param-name
  value: $(path.to.value)
```

You can define new parameters to be used by your templates by accessing the JSON body from an incoming request using **JSONPath** expressions.

Event listeners

The last object created during Tekton Triggers installation is the **EventListener**. As the name implies, the event listener listens for incoming HTTP requests with a JSON payload and will apply a trigger template once this route is reached.

You can see in the following YAML description how the trigger is described. Notice how it links the binding and the template:

```
apiVersion: triggers.tekton.dev/v1alpha1
kind: EventListener
metadata:
  name: listener
spec:
  serviceAccountName: tekton-triggers-example-sa
  triggers:
    - name: trigger-name
      bindings:
        - ref: binding-name
      template:
        ref: template-name
      interceptors:
        ...
```

The event listener will also associate a trigger binding with a trigger template to create an addressable **sink** to which the events are directed.

Summary

In this chapter, you have learned about Tekton Triggers and what it can do to help you automate your CD pipeline. You've also learned about the new objects that Triggers will add to your Kubernetes cluster.

Then, you proceeded to install those CRDs in your cluster and added the necessary tooling for you to expose some new routes that will listen for GitHub webhooks.

In the next chapter, you will see how to use those objects to create your event listeners and connect them to your GitHub repository to automate your pipelines.

11
Triggering Tekton

Now that you know how Tekton Triggers can help you automate your CI/CD pipelines, it is time to put this knowledge to good use. Adding a trigger to start your pipelines automatically is the last step to build a truly automated deployment of your applications.

In this chapter, you will start by creating a simple pipeline. The goal of this pipeline will be to demonstrate that the pipeline can be triggered when you push a new commit to your code repository. Once you have added this pipeline to your cluster, you will see how to create a template, binding, and event listener to listen for GitHub webhooks.

Then, you will need to configure a code repository to connect to your cluster whenever a push event happens. After that, you will be able to test everything out and see how the pipeline is triggered.

In this chapter, we are going to cover the following main topics:

- Creating a pipeline to be triggered
- Creating the trigger
- Configuring incoming webhooks
- Triggering the pipeline

Technical requirements

You can find all of the examples described in this chapter in the chapter-11 folder of the Git repository:

https://github.com/PacktPublishing/Building-CI-CD-systems-using-Tekton

You can also see the code in action videos at the following link: https://bit.ly/3rDOX26

Creating a pipeline to be triggered

To test out your triggers, you will first need a pipeline that can be triggered. By now, you should have a pretty good knowledge of how to build your pipelines. In this pipeline, you will use the same task as the one called logger that you built in *Chapter 5*, *Jumping into Pipelines*. Let's now create a new file called pipeline.yaml, which will contain the following task:

```yaml
apiVersion: tekton.dev/v1beta1
kind: Task
metadata:
  name: logger
spec:
  params:
    - name: text
      type: string
  steps:
    - name: log
      image: registry.access.redhat.com/ubi8/ubi-minimal
      script: |
        DATE=$(date +%d/%m/%Y\ %T)
        echo [$DATE] - $(params.text)
```

The pipeline itself will have a single task that will output the repository name that triggered this pipeline. It will have a single parameter named `repository`, which you will use in the `log-push` task. Add the `---` separator to your `pipeline.yaml` file and then add the following pipeline definition:

```yaml
apiVersion: tekton.dev/v1beta1
kind: Pipeline
metadata:
  name: something-pushed
spec:
  params:
    - name: repository
      type: string
  tasks:
    - name: log-push
      taskRef:
        name: logger
      params:
        - name: text
          value: A push happened in $(params.repository)
```

Once the pipeline is created, you can apply it to your cluster:

```
$ kubectl apply -f ./pipeline.yaml
task.tekton.dev/logger configured
pipeline.tekton.dev/something-pushed created
```

Start a pipeline run to test the output of this pipeline. You should be asked for the repository name as a parameter; add in any value:

```
$ tkn pipeline start something-pushed --showlog
? Value for param `repository` of type `string`? myrepo
PipelineRun started: something-pushed-run-w5bkj
Waiting for logs to be available...
[log-push : log] [06/05/2021 11:34:20] - A push happened in
myrepo
```

You can see that the pipeline worked and logged a single line indicating the repository that was passed as a parameter. The goal now will be to automatically trigger this pipeline on a code push and output the repository name that started the pipeline. In the next section, you will see how to prepare your trigger to listen to these events.

Creating the trigger

In this section, you will learn how to create your first trigger. This trigger will listen for GitHub webhooks and automatically start the pipeline you've just built.

As you now know, you will need three components to set up your triggers. The first new object you will create here is the trigger binding.

TriggerBinding

When GitHub sends a request to your cluster, you will need to extract some of the information sent to convert it to a parameter used by the trigger template.

> **Webhook payloads**
>
> As you build more complex pipelines, you might want to extract more information from the webhook than just the repository name. You might want to check the branch on which the push was done or the name of the committer. You can find the full definition of the webhook payloads on the GitHub documentation site at `https://docs.github.com/en/developers/webhooks-and-events/webhook-events-and-payloads#push`.

In a new file named `binding.yaml`, start by adding the fields that specify the type of object you want to create in your cluster. In this case, it is `TriggerBinding`, based on the `triggers.tekton.dev/v1alpha1` API:

```
apiVersion: triggers.tekton.dev/v1alpha1
kind: TriggerBinding
```

Next, add some metadata. You could add labels to help with future maintenance and cleanup, but for now, we will focus on the essentials pieces and only provide it with a name. You can call this binding `event-binding`:

```
metadata:
  name: event-binding
```

For the `spec` field, you will define a list of parameters. In this particular case, you will describe a single parameter named `git-repository-url`. This parameter will bind to the object found in the JSON body under the `repository.url` property:

```
spec:
  params:
    - name: git-repository-url
      value: $(body.repository.url)
```

You now have your trigger binding. Using this with your event listener, you will be able to use the Git repository URL as a parameter in your trigger template.

TriggerTemplate

Your trigger template will describe the pipeline run to create when you receive an incoming request to your event listener. For this template, you will start the `something-pushed` pipeline you defined at the beginning of this chapter.

Start with a new file called `template.yaml`. In here, create an object of kind `TriggerTemplate`. You can give it the name `push-trigger-template`:

```
apiVersion: triggers.tekton.dev/v1alpha1
kind: TriggerTemplate
metadata:
  name: push-trigger-template
```

For the `spec` field, you can start by defining the parameters that you will use with this template. In this case, it has only one, which is the `git-repositry-url` parameter:

```
spec:
  params:
    - name: git-repository-url
      description: The git repository url
```

Next, you will need to describe the pipeline run that you will create in the `resourcetemplates` list. This `PipelineRun` object uses the same syntax as was introduced in *Chapter 5, Jumping into Pipelines*. Note that in the `params` list, you refer to the parameter defined in the trigger template by using the variable substitution `$(tt.params.git-repository-url)`:

```
  resourcetemplates:
    - apiVersion: tekton.dev/v1beta1
```

```
kind: PipelineRun
metadata:
  generateName: something-pushed-
spec:
  pipelineRef:
    name: something-pushed
  params:
    - name: repository
      value: $(tt.params.git-repository-url)
```

Now that you have a template in place, you will need to create the event listener, which will use the binding and the template that you've just defined.

EventListener

This event listener will be in charge of listening for incoming requests from GitHub. Here, you will specify the binding and template to use when a webhook is triggered.

Start with a new file called listener.yaml. In there, create a new object of kind EventListener named listener:

```
apiVersion: triggers.tekton.dev/v1alpha1
kind: EventListener
metadata:
  name: listener
```

In the spec field, specify the service account to be used by this trigger. You created the necessary service account in *Chapter 10, Getting Started with Triggers,* when you applied the rbac.yaml file from the Tekton Triggers repository. This service account is called tekton-triggers-example-sa:

```
spec:
  serviceAccountName: tekton-triggers-example-sa
```

Next, you will need to add a triggers list to the spec field. In here, you will have a single object called trigger. This trigger object is where you will associate the binding, the template, and the interceptor to be used by the trigger:

```
triggers:
  - name: trigger
    bindings:
```

```
template:
interceptors:
```

In the `bindings` list, you can specify the binding that you created earlier called `event-binding`:

```
bindings:
  - ref: event-binding
```

Specify the template to be used, which is the template that you just created called `push-trigger-template`:

```
template:
  ref: push-trigger-template
```

Finally, you need to specify an interceptor. The interceptor will ensure that this trigger only launches the pipeline when a specific secret key is matched and only on the pre-determined events. In this case, use `git-secret` as `secretName` and `secretKey` as `secretToken`. You will create those in the next section. Finally, this interceptor should only be triggered on pushes:

```
interceptors:
  - github:
      secretRef:
        secretName: git-secret
        secretKey: secretToken
      eventTypes:
        - push
```

You now have all the necessary files to configure your trigger. You can apply those files to your cluster:

```
$ kubectl apply -f ./binding.yaml
triggerbinding.triggers.tekton.dev/event-binding created
```

```
$ kubectl apply -f ./template.yaml
triggertemplate.triggers.tekton.dev/ push-trigger-template
created
```

```
$ kubectl apply -f ./listener.yaml
eventlistener.triggers.tekton.dev/listener created
```

In the next section, you will add the necessary configurations and apply everything in your cluster.

Configuring the incoming webhooks

Now that you have the necessary YAML files to create your trigger, you will need a few more configurations to ensure that your cluster is listening. First, you will need to create a secret to be used to validate that the incoming requests. Then, you will need to expose a route so it can be reached from outside of the cluster. You will need the help of ngrok here to make sure that it is also available from the public internet, which you installed in *Chapter 10, Getting Started with Triggers*. Finally, you will need to add a webhook to a GitHub repository. This webhook will connect to your newly created trigger.

Creating a secret

To ensure that your pipeline is not launched every time a robot accidentally hits your trigger URL, you will need to create a secret. You could use any arbitrary string as a key, but it is a good practice to use a random key for each one of your triggers. For this reason, we will be using a random number converted to base64 for our secret:

```
$ export TEKTON_SECRET_TOKEN=${TEKTON_SECRET_TOKEN-$(head -c 24
/dev/random | base64)}
```

Now that you created a secret token and stored it in an environment variable, you can use the kubectl CLI tool to create a secret in your cluster. This secret will contain the token you just created:

```
$ kubectl create secret generic git-secret --from-
literal=secretToken=$TEKTON_SECRET_TOKEN
secret/git-secret created
```

Keep this token close by, as you will need it in the GitHub configuration step.

Exposing a route

When you created your event listener, Tekton Triggers automatically created a new service for you. You can see this service by using the kubectl tool:

```
$ kubectl get services
NAME                              TYPE        CLUSTER-IP
EXTERNAL-IP    PORT(S)      AGE
el-listener                       ClusterIP   10.110.201.48
```

```
<none>         8080/TCP  18m
kubernetes                        ClusterIP  10.96.0.1
<none>         443/TCP   6d6h
```

You now need to ensure that this service can be reached from outside of your cluster. You can do this by using the port-forward command with the kubectl CLI tool:

```
$ kubectl port-forward svc/el-listener 8080
```

Any incoming request on port 8080 on your local machine will now be redirected to this service and potentially trigger the pipeline. You can give it a try by opening a new terminal and using curl:

```
$ curl localhost:8080
{"eventListener":"listener","namespace":"default",
"errorMessage":"Invalid event body format format: unexpected
end of JSON input"}
```

The event listener returned an error message, but that is expected as you have not provided it with the appropriate headers and payload. For now, seeing this error message is good and indicates the event listener is, indeed, listening.

Making the route publicly available

Any incoming requests on your computer are redirected to the event listener, but you need to expose this port to the outside world so that GitHub can access this route. This redirection is done with ngrok.

To expose a port to the public internet, you can use the following command:

```
$ ngrok http 8080
ngrok by @inconshreveable
(Ctrl+C to quit)


Session Status              online
Session Expires             1 hour, 59 minutes
Version                     2.3.40
Region                      United States (us)
Web Interface                http://127.0.0.1:4040
Forwarding                   http://af827e75984e.ngrok.io ->
http://localhost:8080
```

```
Forwarding                          https://af827e75984e.ngrok.io ->
http://localhost:8080
```

Starting this application creates an address on the `ngrok.io` domain (`http://af827e75984e.ngrok.io` in this case). Any incoming requests to this address are now redirected to your event listener. You can try it in your browser, and you should be getting the same error message as seen in the following screenshot:

```
{"eventListener":"listener","namespace":"default","errorMessage":"In
valid event body format format: unexpected end of JSON input"}
```

Figure 11.1 – Accessing the event listener through a browser

With this route now available to the outside world, you are ready to configure your code repository to reach it every time there is a code push.

Configuring your GitHub repository

The final step is to configure your GitHub repository to send those webhooks every time a push occurs to the repository. You can use any GitHub repository for this step. I recommend that you create a new one with a README.md file. Once your repository is ready, click on **Settings**, then on **Webhooks**. This will open up a new screen where you will be able to add a webhook, as seen in the following screenshot:

Figure 11.2 – New webhook from the GitHub settings

In there, click on **Add webhook**. This will open up a new form where you can enter the following information.

- **Payload URL**: This is your ngrok URL.

- **Content type**: Change this to `application/json`.

- **Secret**: Use the secret token you created earlier. You can view your token with the `echo $TEKTON_SECRET_TOKEN` command.

You can see the completed form in the following screenshot:

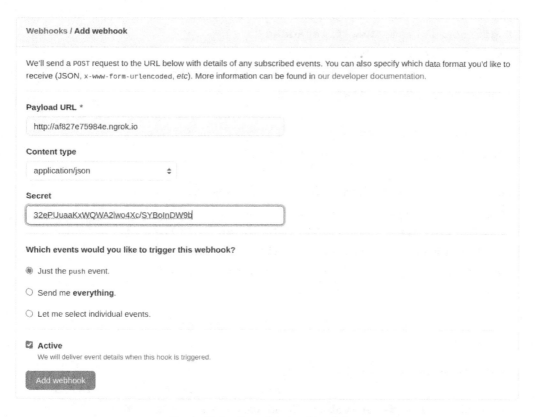

Figure 11.3 – Completed webhook form

Click on **Add webhook** to create the webhook. That is everything you need to get started with your new trigger.

Triggering the pipeline

It's finally time to test out the automation you've put in place. Ensure that you have a clone of your Git repository available on your local machine. From the folder in which the code resides, add a new file:

```
$ touch newfile.txt
```

Now add this file to Git, commit this change, and push the changes to the code repository:

```
$ git add .
```

```
$ git commit -am "New file added"
[main b4c1143] New file added
1 file changed, 0 insertions(+), 0 deletions(-)
create mode 100644 newfile.txt
```

```
$ git push origin main
Enumerating objects: 4, done.
Counting objects: 100% (4/4), done.
Delta compression using up to 8 threads
Compressing objects: 100% (2/2), done.
Writing objects: 100% (3/3), 280 bytes | 280.00 KiB/s, done.
Total 3 (delta 0), reused 0 (delta 0), pack-reused 0
To github.com:joellord/tekton-book-example.git
   6dceaf5..b4c1143 main -> main
```

Now take a look at the list of pipeline runs that have been created so far using the tkn CLI tool:

```
$ tkn pipelinerun ls
NAME                          STARTED         DURATION      STATUS
something-pushed-run-w5bkj    3 minutes ago   7 seconds
Succeeded
something-pushed-run-r7xd8    2 hours ago     15 seconds    Succeeded
```

You should see a new pipeline run that the trigger just created and successfully completed. If you do another change to your repository and push the changes again, you will see a new entry in your list of pipeline runs again.

To ensure that your bindings and templates worked, you can also check out the logs of your most recent run using tkn:

```
$ tkn pipelinerun logs something-pushed-run-w5bkj
[log-push : log] [06/05/2021 11:34:20] - A push happened in
https://github.com/joellord/tekton-book-example
```

This shows that your trigger is correctly configured and now works. Every time some code is changed, it will trigger the pipeline run and perform any operations that you want.

Summary

In this chapter, you've learned how to build and configure your triggers. Using those newly created triggers, you can automate your CI/CD process even more.

You are now more familiar with the structure and usage of trigger templates, trigger bindings, and event listeners. You can use combinations of these objects to customize your triggers in your infrastructure.

You've also seen how you can expose a route from your local system so that you can test out those webhooks that GitHub emits. In a production environment, you will want to use ingresses to expose those services to the outside world. ·

Finally, you made some changes to your repository and were able to see that those changes automatically triggered a pipeline run. That pipeline run had access to some properties from the push event, and in your case, you were able to see the URL of the repository on which the push happened.

You now have everything needed to automate your CI/CD processes. In the next and final part of this book, you will go through the steps of building a pipeline that will automatically deploy an application to your Kubernetes cluster.

Section 4: Putting It All Together

Now that (almost) everything to be said about Tekton has been said, it is time to put all that knowledge into practice and create a pipeline to deploy an application directly from a GitHub repository into a given cluster.

In this section, you will start by resetting your cluster and reinstalling all the necessary components to be able to use Tekton Pipelines and Triggers in your minikube environment. Doing so will act as a refresher on how to install those as well as providing you with a clean slate.

Once your server is ready to go, you will go through the process of creating a full pipeline from scratch that will clone a code base, run some tests on it, build an image, and finally deploy this to your Kubernetes cluster.

By the end of this section, you will understand how to build a full CI/CD system, from scratch, with a real-world example that you can immediately apply to your own projects.

The following chapters are included in this section:

- *Chapter 12, Preparing for a New Pipeline*
- *Chapter 13, Building a Deployment Pipeline*

12
Preparing for a New Pipeline

You've learned everything you need to start building your cloud-native CI/CD pipelines using Tekton. You even know how to automate this process using Tekton Triggers. Up to this point, all the examples were simple. Most of your tasks simply output to the console, and your pipelines didn't have actual use cases.

The time has finally come to start putting everything together and build a real pipeline that you could use in the real world. First, you will start with a clean slate. You will delete everything you have done so far and start with a fresh minikube installation. From there, you will install all the required libraries and get ready to start fresh.

Once your environment is ready, you will clone a code repository and explore the source of an application that is to be deployed in your local cluster. You will then go through the steps of making a change in your code base and deploy the application to your cluster manually. This step will prepare you to understand what is to be automated once you create your pipeline.

In this chapter, we are going to cover the following main topics:

- Cleaning up your cluster
- Installing the necessary tooling
- Exploring the source code

- Deploying the application
- Updating the application manually

Technical requirements

Check out the following link to see the Code in Action video: `https://bit.ly/3eUvkgM`

Cleaning up your cluster

Assuming you are not starting the book at this chapter, your cluster probably has many tasks, pipelines, runs, and other Tekton-related objects in it. To reproduce an authentic environment where you would deploy your pipeline, you will need to start from a clean slate. In this section, you will remove everything you've created so far. In fact, you will go as far as completely deleting your cluster and creating a fresh new one. To do so, from your terminal, stop minikube:

```
$ minikube stop
  Stopping node "minikube" ...
  1 nodes stopped.
```

Once minikube is stopped, you can delete the virtual machine used by minikube to store your Kubernetes cluster. This will ensure that you start from a brand new cluster the next time you start this tool:

```
$ minikube delete
🔥 Deleting "minikube" in kvm2 ...
💀 Removed all traces of the "minikube" cluster.
```

Your cluster has officially been destroyed. You can now restart minikube, just like you did the first time. Using the `start` command will create a fresh new cluster for you to use:

```
$ minikube start
😄 minikube v1.17.1 on Fedora 32
✨ Automatically selected the kvm2 driver. Other choices:
VirtualBox, ssh, podman (experimental)
👍 Starting control plane node minikube in cluster minikube
🔥 Creating kvm2 VM (CPUs=2, Memory=3900MB, Disk=20000MB) ...
🐳 Preparing Kubernetes v1.20.2 on Docker 20.10.2 ...
    * Generating certificates and keys ...
```

```
■*Booting up control plane ...
 * Configuring RBAC rules ...
🔎 Verifying Kubernetes components...
🌟 Enabled add-ons: storage-provisioner, default-storageclass
🦄 Done! kubectl is now configured to use "minikube" cluster
and "default" namespace by default
```

Ensure that the `ingress` add-on is enabled on your cluster by running the `addons` command:

```
$ minikube addons enable ingress
🔎 Verifying ingress addon...
🌟 The 'ingress' addon is enabled
```

You now have a brand new cluster prepared and ready to go. You can ensure that your cluster is empty and that the `kubectl` CLI tool is configured correctly using the `get all` command:

```
$ kubectl get all
NAME TYPE CLUSTER-IP EXTERNAL-IP PORT(S) AGE
service/kubernetes ClusterIP 10.96.0.1 <none> 443/TCP 2m
```

You should only see the Kubernetes service.

Now that you have a new cluster to use, you are ready to reinstall the Tekton **custom resource definitions (CRDs)**.

Installing the necessary tooling

Your cluster is now ready to use, but you should get an error message if you run the `tkn version` command. This error is due to the fact that by deleting everything in your cluster, you also deleted all the CRDs necessary for Tekton.

For this reason, you need to reinstall Tekton, Tekton Triggers, and make some adjustments to your cluster to ensure that you will be able to run those tools.

First, start by installing Tekton by applying the appropriate file to your cluster with `kubectl`:

```
$ kubectl apply --filename https://storage.googleapis.com/
tekton-releases/pipeline/latest/release.yaml
```

Next, install the necessary CRDs for Tekton Triggers using `kubectl`:

```
$ kubectl apply -f https://storage.googleapis.com/tekton-
releases/triggers/latest/release.yaml
```

```
$ kubectl apply -f https://storage.googleapis.com/tekton-
releases/triggers/latest/interceptors.yaml
```

To build your triggers, you will need to create a service account, just like you did previously. In this part, you will be using the same service account that you used earlier. This one was created by applying the following file from the Tekton GitHub repository:

```
$ kubectl apply -f https://raw.githubusercontent.com/tektoncd/
triggers/main/examples/rbac.yaml
```

Finally, you need to make one last adjustment to your cluster to be able to deploy your applications automatically. You will need to give the appropriate role to your service account so that it can access the Kubernetes API and automatically update your application. You can use the following command to do so:

```
$ kubectl create clusterrolebinding serviceaccounts-
cluster-admin --clusterrole=cluster-admin
--group=system:serviceaccounts
```

Your cluster is now up and running with all the necessary tooling to run your Tekton pipelines. You can check that everything was successfully installed with the `tkn` CLI tool:

```
$ tkn version
Client version: 0.17.1
Pipeline version: v0.23.0
Triggers version: v0.13.0
```

Your cluster is ready to receive your application, but before you do so, let's explore this application and see how it can be deployed.

Exploring the source code

You are now ready to deploy your application, but you should know a little bit more about the code you are about to deploy before you do so. While you could use the following pipelines with any Node.js project, it will be easier to follow along if you have the same code samples.

Start by forking the code repository found at `https://github.com/ PacktPublishing/tekton-book-app`. It is crucial that you create your own fork, so you'll be able to add your webhooks to connect to your trigger. Once your fork is ready, clone the repository, and use the `cd` command to get into this new folder:

```
$ git clone git@github.com:<YOUR_USERNAME>/tekton-book-app.
gitgit@github.com:<YOUR_USERNAME>/tekton-book-app.git
Cloning into 'tekton-book-app'...
remote: Enumerating objects: 36, done.
remote: Counting objects: 100% (36/36), done.
remote: Compressing objects: 100% (24/24), done.
remote: Total 36 (delta 14), reused 30 (delta 8), pack-reused 0
Receiving objects: 100% (36/36), 65.39 KiB | 1.31 MiB/s, done.
Resolving deltas: 100% (14/14), done.


$ cd tekton-book-app
```

Feel free to explore the source code of this application with your favorite code editor. This application is a simple web server that uses Express and Node.js. You can find most of the code related to the server in the `server.js` file.

In this `server.js` file, you will see that this server has three routes to which it listens:

- `/` is a route that returns a simple JSON object.
- `/add/:number/:additor` is a route that takes two numbers as parameters and returns the sum.
- `/substract/:number/:substrator` is a route that takes two numbers and returns the difference.

You will also find a `__tests__` folder, which holds the `jest` test suite to test the application. This test suite checks each of the routes to ensure that the return results work. This test suite will need to pass before we deploy our application.

In the root folder of the application, you will see a `.eslintrc.js` file. This file lists the linting rules that should apply to this project. These rules will also need to pass before you deploy the application.

A Dockerfile is present as well. This is the file you will use to create the container to be deployed in your Kubernetes cluster. The file needed to deploy this container into your cluster is called `deploy.yaml` and is also found in the root folder.

Finally, you will find a package.json file that lists all the dependencies for this code base, along with the necessary scripts to run the tests and the code linting.

To start the application, start by installing all the necessary dependencies with the npm tool:

```
$ npm install
```

This operation will take a few seconds and will install all the required packages to run this application. Once this process is completed, you are ready to start the application:

```
$ npm start
> tekton-lab-app@1.0.0 start /home/joel/Code/tekton-lab-app
> node .
Server started on port 3000
```

You can test this application by opening a new terminal window and running the curl command. Using this command, you can test out the three routes on your Express server:

```
$ curl localhost:3000
{"message":"Hello","change":"here"}

$ curl localhost:3000/add/12/10
{"result":22}

$ curl localhost:3000/substract/10/2
{"result":8}
```

Your server is up and running. Before you deploy this application to your cluster, you better ensure that your unit tests are all passing and that your code base is fully linted. Stop the server using *Ctrl + C* and run the following npm commands:

```
$ npm run lint
> tekton-lab-app@1.0.0 lint /home/joel/Code/tekton-lab-app
> eslint *.js

$ npm run test
> tekton-lab-app@1.0.0 test /home/joel/Code/tekton-lab-app
> jest
PASS __tests__/index.js
  Test the root path
```

```
    √ It should answer to GET requests (29 ms)
    √ It should return a Hello message (4 ms)
...

Test Suites: 1 passed, 1 total
Tests: 10 passed, 10 total
Snapshots: 0 total
Time: 1.443 s
Ran all test suites.
```

Seeing that every test passed and no errors showed up, you are ready to deploy your application.

Building and deploying the application

You are now familiar with the code base, and you are confident that all the unit tests are passing. The code is also perfectly linted as no errors came back when you checked. It is now time to deploy this application in your minikube cluster.

To do so, you will need to create an image that you can deploy in your cluster. Once this container has been created, you will push it to an image registry. As part of your Kubernetes deployment, you will then specify the name of the image, and it will be installed directly from the registry.

Creating the container

The Dockerfile to create your container is provided in the root folder of your code base. To build your image with the latest version of the source code, you can use the `docker` CLI tool:

```
$ docker build -t <YOUR_USERNAME>/tekton-lab-app .
STEP 1: FROM node:14
STEP 2: EXPOSE 3000
--> 65f9965b5f9
...
STEP 8: COMMIT <YOUR_USERNAME>/tekton-lab-app
--> 6c61565202a
6c61565202a7b125622a6fb080d1e046995803a
d53bc2771d90113bb214b6c84
```

Now that your image is created, you can ensure that you are logged in to Docker Hub using the `docker login` command. If you are not, Docker will ask you for your credentials:

```
$ docker login docker.io
Authenticating with existing credentials...
Existing credentials are valid. Already logged in to docker.io
```

You may now push your image to the Docker registry:

```
$ docker push <YOUR_USERNAME>/tekton-lab-app
Getting image source signatures
Copying blob 607d71c12b77 skipped: already exists
...
Copying config 6c61565202 done
Writing manifest to image destination
Storing signatures
```

With this newly created container, you will be able to deploy your application in your Kubernetes cluster.

Deploying the application

The image is now stored on Docker Hub and will be accessible to your deployment in your Kubernetes cluster. For your convenience, the whole YAML file needed to deploy and expose your application is provided in the file called `deploy.yaml`. Before you apply this file, make sure that you change the line in the `Deployment` object that specifies the name of the image. This field should refer to your image:

```
apiVersion: apps/v1
kind: Deployment
...
  spec:
    containers:
      - name: tekton-pod
        image: <YOUR_USERNAME>/tekton-lab-app
        ports:
          - containerPort: 3000
```

Once the `Deployment` object has been modified, you are ready to apply this file to your local cluster using `kubectl`:

```
$ kubectl apply -f ./deploy.yaml
deployment.apps/tekton-deployment created
service/tekton-svc created
ingress.networking.k8s.io/tekton-ingress created
```

The application is now up and running in your local minikube cluster. An ingress was also created so that you can access this application from outside of the cluster. You can test that the application is indeed up and running using `curl`:

```
$ curl $(minikube ip)
{"message":"Hello","change":"here"}
```

You can see your application in action, now running in your Kubernetes cluster. The initial deployment was somewhat long to do. Let's see the steps to deploy the application again manually.

Updating the application manually

Now that the application is up and running in a Kubernetes cluster, it is time to change the code base and update this application with the new version. Doing this update by hand will help you identify the parts that you can automate.

First, make a change in a file. Change the response to the `"/"` route in `server.js` to return a different response:

```
app.get("/", (req, res) => {
  res.send({
    message: "Hello",
    change: "changed"
  }).status(200);
});
```

Commit that change and push it to your code repository:

```
$ git commit -am "Change a server response"


$ git push origin main
```

Run the tests and linting to ensure that everything passes:

```
$ npm run test
```

```
$ npm run lint
```

Build a new image and push it to your registry:

```
$ docker build -t <YOUR_USERNAME>/tekton-lab-app .
```

```
$ docker push <YOUR_USERNAME>/tekton-lab-app
```

> **Best practices**
>
> In a production environment, you should always use a new unique tag when building new images. This will avoid running into potential conflicts later down the road. We intentionally omitted the tag here for the sake of simplicity.

Roll out the new version of your application in your cluster:

```
$ kubectl rollout restart deployment/tekton-deployment
```

Test out the new application:

```
$ curl $(minikube ip)
{"message":"Hello","change":"changed"}
```

> **Best practices**
>
> We chose to use the kubectl rollout here for simplicity. In your production environment, it is a better practice to use a declarative syntax, such as kubectl apply. You can find out more about declarative versus imperative syntax in the Kubernetes official documentation at https://kubernetes.io/docs/tasks/manage-kubernetes-objects/.

There you have it. These are the steps to push a new version of your application to your cluster. Ideally, those are the steps that you should automate.

Summary

In this chapter, you've explored the code base for the application for which you will write a CI/CD pipeline. You've seen how this application has a test suite and some linting that should be done before deploying a new version.

You have also seen how to use Docker to build the image and then use `kubectl` to deploy this image to your cluster.

The most critical part of this chapter was the last section. In there, you saw the manual steps that are needed to deploy a new version of this application to your cluster. Of these steps, it is easy for someone to neglect running the test suite and accidentally push some broken code into your cluster. This is why automating these steps is crucial to deploying code faster.

In the next chapter, you will see how to build your Tekton CI/CD pipeline to automate this process.

13
Building a Deployment Pipeline

You are almost there. It is now time to build your first complete CI/CD pipeline to automate your application deployment in your minikube cluster. In the previous chapter, you saw how to deploy the application manually. In this one, you will create all the necessary components to automate this deployment.

First, you will start by analyzing the required steps and determining the necessary components to build your pipelines. Once you have decided on the tasks that you will need for your pipeline, you will need to write those tasks. Thankfully, some tasks are already available for you to use, and you will learn about the Tekton Catalog and how it can help you here.

For most of your tasks, you will be able to use some pre-written ones from the official catalog, yet you will still need to write at least one. This will act as a good refresher on authoring your own tasks.

Finally, once you've established your parameters and workspaces and added all of your tasks, you will be able to write your pipeline. You will then be able to trigger this pipeline to launch your application deployment manually.

Manually starting the pipeline is not ideal, though. The ultimate goal is to automate the launch of this pipeline with every code push that you do. You will achieve this by adding a trigger to your repository.

By the end of this chapter, you will have built a complete automated pipeline to deploy your application in a Kubernetes cluster.

In this chapter, we are going to cover the following main topics:

- Identifying the components
- Using the task catalog
- Adding an additional task
- Creating the pipeline
- Creating the trigger

Technical requirements

You can find all of the examples described in this chapter in the `chapter-13` folder of the Git repository:

`https://github.com/PacktPublishing/Building-CI-CD-systems-using-Tekton`

You can also see the Code in Action videos at the following link: `https://bit.ly/3ybaLV6`

Identifying the components

Before writing your pipeline, the first step is to identify the various components required for your deployment. This step will help you decide the necessary tasks and the order in which they should occur.

Let's think about what operations are needed every time you perform a commit on your source code:

1. **Clone the repository**: The CI/CD pipeline will need a fresh copy of your code base to prepare the next steps.

2. **Install the required libraries**: The containers that are running the testing and linting processes will need to download the necessary modules to perform these operations.

3. **Test the code**: The test suite should be executed and halt the deployment process if the tests do not pass.

4. **Lint the code**: The code should follow the coding standards for this project, or the application should not be allowed to be deployed.

5. **Build and push the image**: Build a container image and push it to a registry.

6. **Deploy the application**: Force Kubernetes to use the latest image and restart the pods.

These actions will each translate into their own task. The order in which the tasks will happen is also critical in this case. The clone operation needs to run first for the other tasks to be able to use the code base. The install task will need to run before the testing and linting steps since those two require some additional modules to be installed. The build and push step should only occur if the testing and linting were both successful. Finally, the deploy step should happen once the image is successfully pushed to the registry.

Now that the tasks and the order in which they should run have been determined, it is time to analyze whether there are any additional components needed.

In this case, you will need to share the code base across all the different steps. For this purpose, you will need a single workspace shared across all of your tasks. The workspace used here will be using a volume claim template defined in the pipeline run.

It would be best if you also aimed at making this pipeline as reusable as possible. To do so, you will need to find out what you can add as a parameter. Should you want to use this pipeline with a different project, you would need to change the source repository. The name of the image and the credentials for the image registry should also be passed in as parameters. Finally, you will need to specify the deployment's name in your cluster that this pipeline should restart once the new image has been pushed. Those five variables will be the parameters that are used for your pipeline.

With all of this in mind, your final pipeline should look as in the following figure:

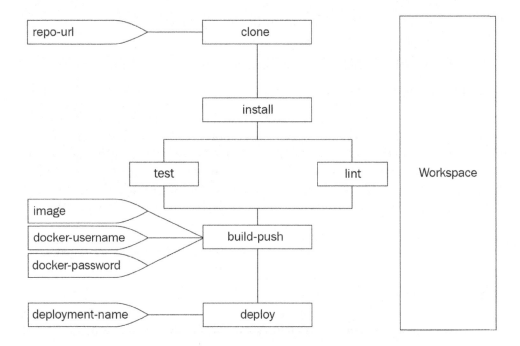

Figure 13.1 – The final pipeline

Now that you know the components needed for your pipeline, it is time to get started adding those tasks.

Using the task catalog

So far, you've created all of your tasks from scratch, but here's a little secret that's been kept from you all this time. There is a list of tasks available out there that are well tested and available for you to use in your pipelines. This list of tasks is called Tekton Hub and was just released out of beta recently. You can access Tekton Hub at `https://hub.tekton.dev`.

Tasks are meant to be reusable whenever possible. For this reason, it makes sense that operations such as a `git clone` have a pre-written task in the catalog. Using such tasks makes it much easier to write your pipeline, as you don't need to reinvent the wheel every time you need a new, common task.

By using the text box in the upper-right corner, you can search for tasks. Clicking on the matching card will open up a description of the task, along with the installation instructions and usage.

Even better, you can install tasks from Tekton Hub directly by using the `tkn` CLI tool. Most of the tasks that you will need for this pipeline are available in the hub. You can go ahead and install them by running the following commands:

```
$ tkn hub install task git-clone
Task git-clone(0.3) installed in default namespace


$ tkn hub install task npm
Task npm(0.1) installed in default namespace


$ tkn hub install task kubernetes-actions
Task kubernetes-actions(0.2) installed in default namespace
```

With these new tasks available in your cluster, you will be able to add the `clone`, `install`, `test`, `lint`, and `deploy` tasks of your pipeline. The only task that is not available is `build-push`, which will need to be manually created.

Adding an additional task

For the `build-push` task, you could've tried to use the `docker build` task, but the image used relies on binding a socket to the Docker daemon, which might not work in all environments. Instead, you will write your task using the **Buildah** tool (https://buildah.io/) to build and push the image to a registry. This image does not require access to the Docker daemon and will work in any context.

For this task, you will have three parameters. The name of the image to be built and pushed should be provided, along with the credentials to connect to the appropriate image registry.

This task will also need a workspace that will contain the source code that should be packaged up as an image.

Finally, the task will have a single step to build the image, log in to the registry, and push the image to it. These operations will require privileged access in the container, so you will also need to specify this in the step description.

First, start with a new task definition in a file named `task.yaml`:

```
apiVersion: tekton.dev/v1beta1
kind: Task
metadata:
  name: build-push
```

In the `spec` field, define your parameters and the workspace:

```
spec:
  params:
    - name: image
    - name: username
    - name: password
  workspaces:
    - name: source
```

For the list of steps, add a single item named `build-image` that uses the `quay.io/buildah/stable:v1.18.0` image. This container will need privileged access:

```
steps:
  - name: build-image
    image: quay.io/buildah/stable:v1.18.0
    securityContext:
      privileged: true
```

Once the container has started, you will need to run the following script, which builds an image, logs in to Docker Hub, and pushes the image:

```
    script: |
    cd $(workspaces.source.path)
    buildah bud --layers -t $(params.image) .
    buildah login -u $(params.username) -p $(params. password)
docker.io
    buildah push $(params.image)
```

You can apply this file to your cluster using `kubectl`:

```
$ kubectl apply -f ./task.yaml
task.tekton.dev/build-push created
```

Your new task is now part of your cluster, and you are ready to write your entire pipeline.

Creating the pipeline

You are now ready to write your new pipeline that will take your source code, run testing and linting, build the image, push it to a registry, and do a rollout on your Kubernetes cluster. It might sound like a lot of work, but let's look at it step by step.

Start with a new file called `pipeline.yaml`. In there, create a new pipeline named `tekton-deploy`:

```yaml
apiVersion: tekton.dev/v1beta1
kind: Pipeline
metadata:
  name: tekton-deploy
```

In the `spec` field, add the parameters and workspace that will be needed for your tasks:

```yaml
spec:
  params:
    - name: repo-url
    - name: deployment-name
    - name: image
    - name: docker-username
    - name: docker-password
  workspaces:
    - name: source
```

Create your `tasks` list and add a first task called `clone`. This task refers to the `git-clone` task and will use the `repo-url` parameter and the `source` workspace. You can find the exact usage for this task on the Tekton Hub website:

```yaml
tasks:
  - name: clone
    taskRef:
      name: git-clone
    params:
      - name: url
        value: $(params.repo-url)
    workspaces:
```

```
    - name: output
      workspace: source
```

Now that you have your source code, you will need to install the dependencies. You will install these in a task called `install`, which uses the npm task. This task uses the same workspace used by the `git-clone` task and needs to run after the `clone` operation:

```
- name: install
  taskRef:
    name: npm
  params:
    - name: ARGS
      value:
        - ci
  workspaces:
    - name: source
      workspace: source
  runAfter:
    - clone
```

Next, you can add a task called `lint`. This task will also use the npm task and the same workspace, and will need to run after the `install` task:

```
- name: lint
  taskRef:
    name: npm
  params:
    - name: ARGS
      value:
        - run
        - lint
  workspaces:
    - name: source
      workspace: source
  runAfter:
    - install
```

The task called `test` will use the same syntax as the `lint` task. It can also be performed after the installation step to run in parallel with the `lint` task:

```
- name: test
  taskRef:
    name: npm
  params:
    - name: ARGS
      value:
        - run
        - test
  workspaces:
    - name: source
      workspace: source
  runAfter:
    - install
```

Next, you are ready to use the `build-push` task you've created to build the image and push it to the registry. Pass in the `image`, `docker-username`, and `docker-password` parameters from the pipeline. You will use the same workspace as all the other tasks. This task will run only if both the `test` and `lint` tasks have been executed successfully:

```
- name: build-push
  taskRef:
    name: build-push
  params:
    - name: image
      value: $(params.image)
    - name: username
      value: $(params.docker-username)
    - name: password
      value: $(params.docker-password)
  workspaces:
    - name: source
      workspace: source
  runAfter:
```

```
      - test
      - lint
```

Finally, add a `deploy` task that will use the `kubernetes-action` task from Tekton Hub. This task will launch the `kubectl rollout` command to download the new image and restart the pods for your application. This task needs to run after the `build-push` one to ensure that the new image is available to be pulled:

```
- name: deploy
  taskRef:
    name: kubernetes-actions
  params:
    - name: args
      value:
        - rollout
        - restart
        - deployment/$(params.deployment-name)
  runAfter:
    - build-push
```

Your pipeline is ready to be used. You can apply it to your cluster with the `kubectl` tool:

```
$ kubectl apply -f ./pipeline.yaml
```

Now that the pipeline is ready, you will need to create the trigger and configure your repository to launch the pipeline automatically.

Creating the trigger

With your pipeline ready, you need to set up your trigger to automatically start the pipeline when someone pushes code to your repository. This trigger will be very similar to the one you wrote in *Chapter 11, Triggering Tekton*.

Start by creating your secret key, which will be shared between your trigger and GitHub:

```
$ export TEKTON_SECRET=$(head -c 24 /dev/random | base64)

$ kubectl create secret generic git-secret --from-
literal=secretToken=$TEKTON_SECRET
```

Note this secret key somewhere, as you will need it later to configure your GitHub webhook. If you need to see it again later, you can use the `echo` command:

```
$ echo $TEKTON_SECRET
```

To add a Tekton trigger to your cluster, you will need three components. You can put all of them in a single file called `trigger.yaml`.

Start with a trigger binding. This binding will be named `event-binding` and will bind the `repository.url` object from the JSON payload to the `gitrepositoryurl` parameter:

```
apiVersion: triggers.tekton.dev/v1alpha1
kind: TriggerBinding
metadata:
  name: event-binding
spec:
  params:
    - name: gitrepositoryurl
      value: $(body.repository.url)
```

Use the separators and add a trigger template. This template, named `commit-tt`, will describe the pipeline run to be created when this event is triggered. Make sure that you edit the values passed as parameters to your actual image name and Docker credentials. The pipeline run will use a volume claim template as a workspace to share the source code across the tasks. This way, you won't need to clean up the workspace when completed:

```
---
apiVersion: triggers.tekton.dev/v1alpha1
kind: TriggerTemplate
metadata:
  name: commit-tt
spec:
  params:
    - name: gitrepositoryurl
      description: The git repository url
  resourcetemplates:
    - apiVersion: tekton.dev/v1beta1
      kind: PipelineRun
      metadata:
```

```
        generateName: tekton-deploy-
    spec:
        pipelineRef:
          name: tekton-deploy
        params:
          - name: repo-url
            value: $(tt.params.gitrepositoryurl)
          - name: deployment-name
            value: tekton-deployment
          - name: image
            value: <YOUR_USERNAME>/tekton-lab-app
          - name: docker-username
            value: <YOUR_USERNAME>
          - name: docker-password
            value: <YOUR_PASSWORD>
        workspaces:
          - name: source
            volumeClaimTemplate:
              spec:
                accessModes:
                  - ReadWriteOnce
                resources:
                  requests:
                    storage: 1Gi
```

Finally, use another separator and add your event listener named `listener`. This event listener will use your trigger template and trigger binding that you've just created:

```
---
apiVersion: triggers.tekton.dev/v1alpha1
kind: EventListener
metadata:
  name: listener
spec:
  serviceAccountName: tekton-triggers-example-sa
triggers:
  - name: trigger
```

```
      bindings:
        - ref: event-binding
      template:
        ref: commit-tt
      interceptors:
        - github:
            secretRef:
              secretName: git-secret
              secretKey: secretToken
            eventTypes:
              - push
```

Now that everything is in place, you are ready to apply this file to your cluster:

```
$ kubectl apply -f ./trigger.yaml
triggerbinding.triggers.tekton.dev/event-binding created
triggertemplate.triggers.tekton.dev/commit-tt created
eventlistener.triggers.tekton.dev/listener created
```

Now, expose that event listener and run `ngrok` to create a public route to your local Kubernetes cluster:

```
$ kubectl port-forward svc/el-listener 8080


$ ngrok http 8080
```

The last step is to go to GitHub and add a new webhook to your repository. From the **Add webhook** screen in GitHub, fill in the form with the following values:

- **Payload URL**: This is your public `ngrok` URL.
- **Content Type**: This should be changed to `application/json`.
- **Secret**: This is the secret you've stored in the `$TEKTON_SECRET` environment variables.

Leave the default values for the other fields.

You are now ready to test out everything. Make a change in your `tekton-lab-app` project. Then, commit that change and push the code back to your repository. After a few seconds, try to list the pipeline runs in your cluster using the `tkn` CLI tool:

```
$ tkn pipelineruns ls
NAME                        STARTED          DURATION    STATUS
tekton-deploy-z89gr         2 seconds ago    ---         Running
```

You should see that a new pipeline run was recently started and either be running or marked as completed. If you've changed the response to one of the routes defined in `server.js`, you should be able to contact your local cluster with `curl` and see the changes now deployed in your cluster.

Summary

In this chapter, you've built your first complete pipeline that will have an actual use case. Starting from scratch, you've seen how to plan for your task, parameters, and workspaces.

With this plan in hand, you could use the knowledge you've got from this book to build a complete pipeline. Starting from the Tekton Hub tasks, you could reuse some components that the Tekton community has created. You have also made a task that you used in the pipeline. You've then created a large pipeline that reproduces all the steps you did manually in the previous chapter to deploy your application.

Ultimately, you created a trigger so that this pipeline would automatically start every time some code is pushed to your repository. This pipeline is still somewhat simple. With what you've learned across this book, you can make it your own and build on top of it.

For example, if you need different tasks based on the branch that someone made the push on, you could use when expressions, just like you learned in *Chapter 8*, *Adding when Expressions*. If you wanted to connect to a private repository to clone the code, you could use authentication, as you did in *Chapter 9*, *Securing Authentication*.

Good job! You have all the necessary tooling to create robust Tekton pipelines; it is up to you to put this knowledge together and start building your CI/CD systems using Tekton. Thank you for tagging along all the way through this book. Tekton is evolving really fast as it is getting closer and closer to an official release. If you want to learn more, I strongly recommend that you keep an eye on the official website at `http://tekton.dev`. The documentation is well updated and should provide you with even more information about advanced concepts and examples.

Assessments

Some chapters across the book had exercises for you to practice and improve your Tekton Pipelines authoring skills. In this section, you will find the solutions to those exercises. Your own implementation might vary, but these examples should provide you with enough context to fine-tune your own answers.

The solutions are printed here for easy reference, or you can find them in GitHub, as described in the next section.

Technical requirements

You can find all of the examples described in this chapter in the `assessments` folder of the Git repository at `https://github.com/PacktPublishing/Building-CI-CD-systems-using-Tekton`.

Chapter 4

This chapter was all about tasks, and so are these exercises. The goal of these exercises is to let you become familiar with the basic concepts around steps and tasks.

More than Hello World

In this first challenge, build a task with three steps. The first step should output a log message stating that the task has started. Then, the task will sleep for the number of seconds that the user specifies. In the third step, the task should log a string that the user provides. Be sure to add default values to those two parameters. Now, try running the task with the `tkn` **command-line interface (CLI)** tool. Run it a second time using the default values this time. Start this task a third time, specifying the parameter values directly in the command line.

Here is a possible solution for the exercise:

```yaml
apiVersion: tekton.dev/v1beta1
kind: Task
metadata:
  name: more-than-hello
spec:
  params:
    - name: log
      type: string
      default: Done sleeping
    - name: pause-duration
      type: string
      default: "1"
  steps:
    - name: greet
      image: registry.access.redhat.com/ubi8/ubi-minimal
      command:
        - /bin/bash
      args: ['-c', 'echo Welcome to this task']
    - name: pause
      image: registry.access.redhat.com/ubi8/ubi-minimal
      command:
        - /bin/bash
      args: ['-c', 'sleep $(params.pause-duration)']
    - name: log
      image: registry.access.redhat.com/ubi8/ubi-minimal
      command:
        - /bin/bash
      args: ['-c', 'echo $(params.log)']
```

Build a generic curl task

For this challenge, build a task that will use the curl application to fetch some information about a web page. The user should pass in any argument that can be used with curl, along with the **Uniform Resource Locator** (**URL**) to reach. The output of curl should be produced in a separate task.

Here is a possible solution for the exercise:

```yaml
apiVersion: tekton.dev/v1beta1
kind: Task
metadata:
  name: curl
spec:
  results:
    - name: response
      description: Response from cURL
  params:
    - name: url
      description: URL to cURL
      type: string
    - name: args
      description: Additional arguments
      type: array
      default: []
  steps:
    - name: curl
      image: registry.access.redhat.com/ubi8/ubi
      command:
        - curl
      args:
        - $(params.args[*])
        - -o
        - $(results.response.path)
        - --url
        - $(params.url)
    - name: output
      image: registry.access.redhat.com/ubi8/ubi
      script: |
        echo Output from the cURL to $(params.url)
        cat $(results.response.path)
```

Create a random user

For this challenge, create a task that will make a request to the Random User **application programming interface (API)** (`http://randomuser.me`) and extract the first and last name of the random user that was generated. A `nat` parameter to specify the randomly generated user's nationality should be specified in a ConfigMap.

Here is a possible solution for the exercise:

```yaml
apiVersion: v1
kind: ConfigMap
metadata:
  name: randomuser
data:
  nationality: gb
---
apiVersion: tekton.dev/v1beta1
kind: Task
metadata:
  name: randomuser
spec:
  volumes:
    - name: nationality
      configMap:
        name: randomuser
  results:
    - name: config
      description: Configuration file for cURL
    - name: output
      description: Output from curl
  steps:
    - name: config
      image: registry.access.redhat.com/ubi8/ubi
      volumeMounts:
        - name: nationality
          mountPath: /var/nat
      script: |
        echo "url=https://randomuser.me/
api/?inc=name,nat&nat="$(cat /var/nat/nationality) > $(results.
```

```
config.path)
    - name: curl
      image: registry.access.redhat.com/ubi8/ubi
      command:
        - curl
      args:
        - -K
        - $(results.config.path)
        - -o
        - $(results.output.path)
  - name: output
    image: stedolan/jq
    script: |
        FIRST=$(cat $(results.output.path) | jq -r .results[0].
name.first)
        LAST=$(cat $(results.output.path) | jq -r .results[0].
name.last)
        NAT=$(cat $(results.output.path) | jq -r .results[0].
nat)
        echo "New random user created with nationality $NAT"
        echo $FIRST $LAST
```

Chapter 5

In this chapter, you learned about pipelines. The goal of the following exercises is to help you improve your pipeline authoring skills.

Back to the basics

For your first challenge, start by building a pipeline that will output a hello message. To do so, use the logger task that you created in this chapter. The pipeline will take a parameter to indicate who to say hello to, and this should default to World. Run this pipeline with different parameter values using the CLI. Then, run it with the default values. Do one last run with the parameter value specified in the CLI command directly. Here is a possible solution for the exercise:

```
apiVersion: tekton.dev/v1beta1
kind: Pipeline
metadata:
```

```
  name: back-to-basics
spec:
  params:
    - name: who
      default: "World"
      type: string
      description: Who should we say hello to?
  tasks:
    - name: say-hello
      params:
        - name: text
          value: Hello $(params.who)
      taskRef:
        name: logger
```

Counting files in a repo

For this next challenge, build a pipeline that will clone a Git repository and then output the number of files found in that repository. Use the logger task to output the number of files.

Here is a possible solution for the exercise:

```
apiVersion: tekton.dev/v1beta1
kind: Task
metadata:
  name: clone-and-count
spec:
  params:
    - name: repo
      type: string
  results:
    - name: file-count
      description: Number of files
  steps:
    - name: clone-and-ls
      image: alpine/git
      script: |
```

```
            git clone $(params.repo) .
            ls | wc -l > $(results.file-count.path)
---
apiVersion: tekton.dev/v1beta1
kind: Pipeline
metadata:
  name: count-files
spec:
  params:
    - name: repo-to-analyze
  tasks:
    - name: get-list
      taskRef:
        name: clone-and-count
      params:
        - name: repo
          value: $(params.repo-to-analyze)
    - name: output-count
      taskRef:
        name: logger
      params:
        - name: text
          value: "Number of files in $(params.repo-to-analyze):
$(tasks.get-list.results.file-count)"
      runAfter:
        - get-list
```

Weather services

For this last challenge, build a pipeline that gets weather information and outputs only the current temperature. You can use the wttr.in website to get the weather data in a text format that you can then process. The name of the city should be a parameter. You will use the weather-service result in a second task to extract only the current temperature. Finally, use the logger task to output the temperature.

Here is a possible solution for the exercise:

```yaml
apiVersion: tekton.dev/v1beta1
kind: Task
metadata:
  name: weather
spec:
  params:
    - name: city
      type: string
  results:
    - name: weather
      description: JSON object with weather definition
  steps:
    - name: get-weather
      image: registry.access.redhat.com/ubi8/ubi
      script: |
        curl wttr.in/$(params.city)?format=4 -o $(results.weather.path)
---
apiVersion: tekton.dev/v1beta1
kind: Task
metadata:
  name: weather-extract
spec:
  results:
    - name: temperature
      description: Current temperature
  params:
    - name: weather-data
      type: string
  steps:
    - name: extract-data
      image: registry.access.redhat.com/ubi8/ubi
      script: |
        echo "$(params.weather-data)" | awk '{print $3}' > $(results.temperature.path)
```

```
---
apiVersion: tekton.dev/v1beta1
kind: Pipeline
metadata:
  name: weather
spec:
  params:
    - name: city
      type: string
      default: Ottawa
  tasks:
    - name: get-weather
      params:
        - name: city
          value: $(params.city)
      taskRef:
        name: weather
    - name: extract-data
      params:
        - name: weather-data
          value: $(tasks.get-weather.results.weather)
      taskRef:
        name: weather-extract
      runAfter:
        - get-weather
    - name: current-temperature
      params:
        - name: text
          value: Current temperature in $(params.city) is
$(tasks.extract-data.results.temperature)
      taskRef:
        name: logger
      runAfter:
        - extract-data
```

Chapter 6

In this chapter, you learned one important concept called `finally` tasks. In this section, you will put this knowledge to work and use exit codes to change the final output of your pipelines.

Fail if root

Create a pipeline with a simple task. This task will check whether the container is running as the root user. If it is indeed running as the root user, the task will fail.

Here is a possible solution for the exercise:

```
apiVersion: tekton.dev/v1beta1
kind: Task
metadata:
  name: fail-if-root
spec:
  steps:
    - name: fail-if-root
      image: registry.access.redhat.com/ubi8/ubi
      script: |
        if [ $(whoami) == "root" ]
          then
            echo "User is root"
            exit 1
        fi
        exit 0
---
apiVersion: tekton.dev/v1beta1
kind: Pipeline
metadata:
  name: check-root
spec:
  tasks:
    - name: is-root
      taskRef:
        name: fail-if-root
```

Make your bets

Imagine a game of Blackjack. The current hand value is 17. Draw a random card with a value between 1 and 10 and add it to the current hand. The value should be passed to the second task as a result. If the value is 21 or less, you win, and the task should complete successfully. If the value is higher than 21, it should fail. After the game, clean up the table.

Here is a possible solution for the exercise:

```yaml
apiVersion: tekton.dev/v1beta1
kind: Task
metadata:
  name: draw-card
spec:
  results:
    - name: card
      description: Card value
  steps:
    - name: randomize
      image: node:14
      script: |
        #!/usr/bin/env node
        const fs = require("fs");
        const cardValue = Math.floor(Math.random() * 10) + 1;
        fs.writeFileSync("$(results.card.path)", cardValue.toString());
---
apiVersion: tekton.dev/v1beta1
kind: Task
metadata:
  name: check-result
spec:
  params:
    - name: new-card
      type: string
  steps:
    - name: add-card
      image: registry.access.redhat.com/ubi8/ubi
```

```
      script: |
        HAND=17
        NEWCARD=$(params.new-card)
        NEWHAND=$(($HAND+$NEWCARD))
        echo "New hand value is $NEWHAND"
        if (($NEWHAND > 21))
          then
            echo "Busted"
            exit 1
        fi
        echo "You won"
        exit 0
---
apiVersion: tekton.dev/v1beta1
kind: Pipeline
metadata:
  name: make-your-bets
spec:
  tasks:
    - name: draw
      taskRef:
        name: draw-card
    - name: check
      taskRef:
        name: check-result
      params:
        - name: new-card
          value: $(tasks.draw.results.card)
      runAfter:
        - draw
  finally:
    - name: clean
      taskRef:
        name: logger
      params:
```

```
      - name: text
        value: "Cleaning up the table"
```

Chapter 7

In this chapter, you learned how to share large quantities of data across tasks in a pipeline. This will be useful when you start dealing with Git repositories. The following exercises will give you some practice with the concept of workspaces.

Write and read

Create a task that uses a workspace to share information across its two steps. The first step will write a message, specified in a parameter, to a file in the workspace. The second step will output the content of the file in the logs. Try running the task using the -w parameter in the tkn CLI tool.

Here is a possible solution for the exercise:

```
apiVersion: tekton.dev/v1beta1
kind: Task
metadata:
  name: write-read-workspace
spec:
  workspaces:
    - name: data
  params:
    - name: message
      default: "Hello World"
      type: string
      description: "Message to write in the workspace"
  steps:
    - name: write
      image: registry.access.redhat.com/ubi8/ubi
      command:
        - /bin/bash
      args:
        - -c
        - echo "$(params.message)" > $(workspaces.data.path)/
message.txt
```

```
  - name: read
    image: registry.access.redhat.com/ubi8/ubi
    command:
      - /bin/bash
    args:
      - -c
      - cat $(workspaces.data.path)/message.txt
```

Pick a card

Using the Deck of Cards API available at `http://deckofcardsapi.com/`, create a pipeline that will generate a new deck of cards and then pick a single card from it. The first call will generate a `deck` **identifier (ID)** that you can then use in the next task to pick a card. Output the card value and suit in the second task.

Here is a possible solution for the exercise:

```
apiVersion: tekton.dev/v1beta1
kind: Task
metadata:
  name: deck-api-create
spec:
  workspaces:
    - name: deck
  steps:
    - name: create-deck
      image: registry.access.redhat.com/ubi8/ubi
      script: |
        curl https://deckofcardsapi.com/api/deck/new/shuffle/
-o $(workspaces.deck.path)/deck-id.txt
---
apiVersion: tekton.dev/v1beta1
kind: Task
metadata:
  name: deck-api-draw
spec:
  workspaces:
    - name: deck
```

```yaml
  steps:
    - name: draw
      image: node:14
      script: |
        #!/usr/bin/env node
        const fs = require("fs");
        const https = require("https");
        const deck = fs.readFileSync("$(workspaces.deck.path)/
deck-id.txt");
        const deckId = JSON.parse(deck).deck_id;
        const URL = `https://deckofcardsapi.com/api/
deck/${deckId}/draw/`;
        console.log(URL);
        https.get(URL, response => {
          response.on("data", data => {
            let card = JSON.parse(data).cards[0];
            console.log("Card was drawn from the deck");
            console.log(`${card.value} of ${card.suit}`);
          })
        });
---
apiVersion: tekton.dev/v1beta1
kind: Pipeline
metadata:
  name: pick-a-card
spec:
  workspaces:
    - name: api-data
  tasks:
    - name: create-deck
      taskRef:
        name: deck-api-create
      workspaces:
        - name: deck
          workspace: api-data
    - name: pick-card
      taskRef:
```

```
      name: deck-api-draw
  workspaces:
    - name: deck
      workspace: api-data
  runAfter:
    - create-deck
```

Hello admin

Build a pipeline that will return a different greeting, whether the username passed as a parameter is admin or something else. This pipeline should have two tasks. The first task will verify the username and output the role (admin or user) in the result. The second task will pick up this role and display the appropriate message from a ConfigMap mounted as a workspace.

Here is a possible solution for the exercise:

```
apiVersion: v1
kind: ConfigMap
metadata:
  name: messages
data:
  admin-welcome: Welcome master.
  user-welcome: Hello user.
---
apiVersion: tekton.dev/v1beta1
kind: Task
metadata:
  name: get-role
spec:
  results:
    - name: role
  params:
    - name: user
      type: string
  steps:
    - name: check-username
      image: registry.access.redhat.com/ubi8/ubi
```

```
      script: |
        #!/usr/bin/env bash
        if [ "$(params.user)" == "admin" ]; then
          echo "admin" > $(results.role.path)
        else
          echo "user" > $(results.role.path)
        fi
---
apiVersion: tekton.dev/v1beta1
kind: Task
metadata:
  name: role-based-greet
spec:
  params:
    - name: role
      type: string
  workspaces:
    - name: messages
  steps:
    - name: greet
      image: registry.access.redhat.com/ubi8/ubi
      script: |
        ROLE=$(params.role)
        cat $(workspaces.messages.path)/$ROLE-welcome
---
apiVersion: tekton.dev/v1beta1
kind: Pipeline
metadata:
  name: admin-or-not
spec:
  params:
    - name: username
      default: user
      type: string
  workspaces:
    - name: message-map
```

```
tasks:
  - name: validate-admin
    taskRef:
      name: get-role
    params:
      - name: user
        value: $(params.username)
  - name: greetings
    taskRef:
      name: role-based-greet
    params:
      - name: role
        value: $(tasks.validate-admin.results.role)
    workspaces:
      - name: messages
        workspace: message-map
    runAfter:
      - validate-admin
```

Chapter 8

Sometimes, your pipeline will need to execute tasks based on certain conditions. In this chapter, you learned how to use when expressions to add conditional flows to your pipelines. You now have the opportunity to get some experience with this concept here.

Hello Admin

Build a pipeline that will take a username as a parameter. If the username is admin, log the Hello Admin text. For any other username, output a simple Hello message.

Here is a possible solution for the exercise:

```
apiVersion: tekton.dev/v1beta1
kind: Task
metadata:
  name: logger
spec:
  params:
```

```yaml
  - name: text
    type: string
steps:
  - name: log
    image: registry.access.redhat.com/ubi8/ubi-minimal
    script: |
      DATE=$(date +%d/%m/%Y\ %T)
      echo [$DATE] - $(params.text)
---
apiVersion: tekton.dev/v1beta1
kind: Pipeline
metadata:
  name: hello-admin
spec:
  params:
    - name: username
      type: string
  tasks:
    - name: hello-admin
      taskRef:
        name: logger
      params:
        - name: text
          value: "Hello Admin"
      when:
        - input: $(params.username)
          operator: in
          values: ["admin"]
    - name: hello-other
      taskRef:
        name: logger
      params:
        - name: text
          value: "Hello User"
      when:
        - input: $(params.username)
```

```
            operator: notin
            values: ["admin"]
```

Critical Hit

In role-playing games using dice, rolling a 20 on a 20-sided dice is sometimes referred to as rolling a critical hit. For this exercise, build a pipeline that would log Critical Hit when the result of a dice roll is 20. To do so, use a task that will generate a random number between 1 and 20 and produce a result that the when expression of a second task can pick up.

Here is a possible solution for the exercise:

```
apiVersion: tekton.dev/v1beta1
kind: Task
metadata:
  name: dice-roll-result
spec:
  params:
    - name: sides
      type: string
  results:
    - name: dice-roll
      description: Random number generated by the dice roll
  steps:
    - name: generate-random-number
      image: node:14
      script: |
        #!/usr/bin/env node
        const fs = require("fs");
        const max = $(params.sides)
        let randomNumber =  Math.floor(Math.random() * Math.
floor(max)) + 1;
        fs.writeFile("$(results.dice-roll.path)", randomNumber.
toString(), () => {
          console.log("Dice rolled");
        });
---
apiVersion: tekton.dev/v1beta1
```

```
kind: Pipeline
metadata:
  name: results
spec:
  params:
    - name: sides
      default: "20"
      type: "string"
  tasks:
    - name: intro
      params:
        - name: text
          value: "Preparing to roll the $(params.sides)-sided
dice"
      taskRef:
        name: logger
    - name: roll
      params:
        - name: sides
          value: $(params.sides)
      taskRef:
        name: dice-roll-result
      runAfter:
        - intro
    - name: critical
      taskRef:
        name: logger
      params:
        - name: text
          value: "Critical hit!"
      when:
        - input: $(tasks.roll.results.dice-roll)
          operator: in
          values: ["20"]
      runAfter:
        - roll
```

```
    - name: result
      params:
        - name: text
          value: "Result from dice roll was $(tasks.roll.
results.dice-roll)"
      taskRef:
        name: logger
      runAfter:
        - roll
```

Not working on weekends

Even your servers deserve a break. Build a pipeline with a task that Tekton will only execute on weekdays. The task should log a `Working` message to simulate some work.

Here is a possible solution for the exercise:

```
apiVersion: tekton.dev/v1beta1
kind: Task
metadata:
  name: get-day
spec:
  results:
    - name: daynumber
      description: day of week, 0 is Sunday
  steps:
    - name: get-day
      image: registry.access.redhat.com/ubi8/ubi
      script: |
        date +%w | tr -d '\n' > $(results.daynumber.path)
---
apiVersion: tekton.dev/v1beta1
kind: Pipeline
metadata:
  name: not-on-weekends
spec:
  tasks:
    - name: getday
```

```
    taskRef:
      name: get-day
 - name: work
    taskRef:
      name: logger
    params:
      - name: text
        value: Working...
    when:
      - input: $(tasks.getday.results.daynumber)
        operator: in
        values: ["1", "2", "3", "4", "5"]
    runAfter:
      - getday
```

`Packt.com`

Subscribe to our online digital library for full access to over 7,000 books and videos, as well as industry leading tools to help you plan your personal development and advance your career. For more information, please visit our website.

Why subscribe?

- Spend less time learning and more time coding with practical eBooks and Videos from over 4,000 industry professionals

- Improve your learning with Skill Plans built especially for you

- Get a free eBook or video every month

- Fully searchable for easy access to vital information

- Copy and paste, print, and bookmark content

Did you know that Packt offers eBook versions of every book published, with PDF and ePub files available? You can upgrade to the eBook version at `packt.com` and as a print book customer, you are entitled to a discount on the eBook copy. Get in touch with us at `customercare@packtpub.com` for more details.

At `www.packt.com`, you can also read a collection of free technical articles, sign up for a range of free newsletters, and receive exclusive discounts and offers on Packt books and eBooks.

Other Books You May Enjoy

If you enjoyed this book, you may be interested in these other books by Packt:

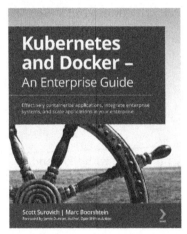

Kubernetes and Docker - An Enterprise Guide

Scott Surovich and Marc Boorshtein

ISBN: 978-1-83921-340-3

- Create a multinode Kubernetes cluster using kind
- Implement Ingress, MetalLB, and ExternalDNS
- Configure a cluster OIDC using impersonation
- Map enterprise authorization to Kubernetes
- Secure clusters using PSPs and OPA

Hands-on Kubernetes on Azure - Third Edition

Nills Franssens, Shivakumar Gopalakrishnan, and Gunther Lenz

ISBN: 978-1-80107-994-5

- Plan, configure, and run containerized applications in production.
- Use Docker to build applications in containers and deploy them on Kubernetes.
- Monitor the AKS cluster and the application.
- Monitor your infrastructure and applications in Kubernetes using Azure Monitor.
- Secure your cluster and applications using Azure-native security tools.

Packt is searching for authors like you

If you're interested in becoming an author for Packt, please visit `authors.packtpub.com` and apply today. We have worked with thousands of developers and tech professionals, just like you, to help them share their insight with the global tech community. You can make a general application, apply for a specific hot topic that we are recruiting an author for, or submit your own idea.

Share your thoughts

Now you've finished *Building CI/CD Systems Using Tekton*, we'd love to hear your thoughts! Scan the QR code below to go straight to the Amazon review page for this book and share your feedback or leave a review on the site that you purchased it from.

`https://packt.link/r/1801078211`

Your review is important to us and the tech community and will help us make sure we're delivering excellent quality content.

Index

Made in the USA
Coppell, TX
21 November 2023